MW00881865

YOUR KID'S REBOUND FROM PANDEMIC LOCKDOWNS

A Parent's Guide to Restoring Their Family

BY JEFF NELLIGAN

Copyright © 2022 Jeff Nelligan

All rights reserved. This book or any portion thereof may not be reproduced or used in any manner whatsoever without the express written permission of the publisher except for the use of brief quotations in a book review.

ISBN: 9798360844747

DEDICATION

To parents and their kids.

Trite and timeless and relentlessly true:
Kids will live up to what you believe of them.

TABLE OF CONTENTS

Disclaimer:
These pages are not intended to provide medical advice or physician or therapist instruction. Information provided should not be used for diagnostic or training purposes. Consult a therapist or physician regarding specific diagnoses or medical advice.

PREFACE

Several years ago I wrote a short book, *Four Lessons From My Three Sons: How You Can Raise Resilient Kids*. It explains the techniques I used as a parent to form my boys' character, the touchstones of which are principled conduct, grinding endurance and resolute confidence. The driving force of my instruction was highlighting real-world situations with people and places that my kids and I encountered on a daily basis. Positive and unusual and negative and sometimes tricky, these experiences played out at school and malls, restaurants and athletic fields, community events and everywhere in between.

Repeatedly thrust into unfamiliar situations day in and day out and having to navigate them (the *Lessons*) helped my sons gradually acquire resilience (hence the title), which I believe is the most important personal quality a kid – or an adult – can possess. In fact, over time my sons become nearly reflexive in managing with confidence most of the ups and downs of childhood and adolescence. Three average young children (1) evolved into sharp, rugged and alert teenagers, characteristics that propelled them to the U.S. Naval Academy, Williams College, West Point and beyond.

The book's authenticity derived from the fact that I was (and remain) an average, middle-class bread-winner - a Parent-Teacher Association-type, a coach and occasional rec league referee, kid shuttle-bus driver and community volunteer and mediocre backyard barbeque guy; yes, a Dad, one who has been closely involved with young boys and girls and their parents for two decades in every venue under the sun known to the American family. (2)

As such, I've had a front row seat in viewing the sometimes stark contrasts in the kid panorama — all the successes that are deserved, heartwarming and pure. But most important for you and this book, I've also seen *all of the setbacks*. I mean <u>all</u> — the maddening academic shortcomings and consequences; the jarring social disappointments and fallouts with peers; the unbelievably stupid hijinks leading to disciplinary actions and public athletic embarrassments; family economic crises and the raw, painful friction with Dad and Mom. My three sons encountered and indeed, sometimes brought upon themselves these trials and while they didn't get over all of them, they drove through the most important. That's the way it is and always will be. Adversity in a kid's life is a constant; no one gets a free ride. I'm not telling you anything don't know or haven't seen.

Nevertheless, one thing is as clear to me as it is to every other parent:

The hardships our kids have endured during the past two years are unprecedented. And making up the lost ground will be the most difficult and important duty a parent undertakes.

Footnotes

1. By average I mean average. Average minds and abilities - no Mensa intellects or scientific and mathematical talents, no outstanding artistic creativity or athletic gifts, no substantial family economic wealth. I know. I was with them every step of the way.

2. The book spent four months in the top-20 Amazon's Parenting Best Sellers list and spurred feature stories on *National Public Radio* and in dozens of parenting publications, including *Parents Magazine, Fatherly, Young Teen Magazine, The Good Men Project, Fatherhood* and *Let Grow.*

THE APPALLING DAMAGE OF PANDEMIC LOCKDOWNS

"When you're going through hell, keep going." Winston Churchill

No generation of youth has borne the peculiar suffering of our children during the Covid-19 pandemic and the resulting lockdowns, school and societal closures, forced confinement, quarantines and the ever-present social fear and foreboding since March 15th of 2020.

That day forward was the onset of an unparalleled separation of young children, pre-teens and teenagers from their heretofore normal life. The now widely accepted consensus is:

1. School closings and online learning combined with the suspension of daily social interaction found in virtually all non-school venues resulted in:

2. Protracted isolation causing significant harm to youths in the areas of mental health and well-being, physical health, and educational progress.

All this is undeniable. It is as simple as I can put it. No kid was left untouched; all were left behind in one way or another.

Not even epic, national shocks - a decade-long national economic Depression or World War II – resulted in the near total seclusion and confinement of our country's young people.

Added to near this near-total isolation was the daily low-grade environment of anxiety – here think of masking and social distancing, daily testing, quarantines and the breathless 24/7 news coverage of cases numbers, hospitalizations, sickness and death.

All this has pushed families to a breaking point and I wager you wouldn't think this hyperbole. In fact, the chapters in this book and its Appendixes are crammed with more than 200 cites to extensive, exhaustive research detailing the damage to children from pandemic lockdowns.

WHAT IS THE CURRENT STATE OF PLAY?

As life starts to resemble pre-pandemic normalcy, beleaguered parents know their kids have to make up lost ground in key facets of their lives. Perhaps these are some questions you're asking yourselves:

- What was the true extent of my child's social, educational, and physical reverses during lockdowns?

- Do I count solely on the remedies put in place by public and private institutions that promise — or hope - to alleviate the damage inflicted on my kid?

- How can I as a parent get my child back on the path to the normal, cheerful, well-adjusted kid they once were?

And perhaps most important:

- Is a return to the pre-pandemic, pre-lockdown behaviors and attitudes of my child good enough? Or is there more I should seek?

WHAT THIS BOOK OFFERS YOU

This slender volume goes a long way in answering those questions. And right now I'll reveal the unfiltered candor you'll find throughout this book: No-one has the full answers. Not the multitude of professionals whose research you will find here, not this Dad, and not you.

What this book *does* provide is a way forward; as the title states, a *Rebound*.

First and important, it relies on hard facts and data and the advice and guidance of the nation's leading parenting and family experts and medical and psychological authorities.

To be clear: The cites are not here to prove your author, a perennial C student, is a scholar. They are here to provide the incontrovertible truths that the damage was real and fully documented.

Combined, the chapters here detail what happened during lock-downs and what parents can do to reinvigorate their kids' lives.

Second, while no book is unique, this book does one thing well: It contains a wealth of information, drawn from hundreds of expert sources, *in consolidated fashion*. Here is the best thinking on how to guide the development of children - whether they are young, pre-teens or adolescents - in this post-lockdown period. It is succinctly organized and written by a parent with the busy parent in mind.

Third, at points I offer personal observations from my experience (explained in the Preface) as a parent myself.

WARNING: WHAT'S NOT IN THIS BOOK...

...Sincere but over-the-top sentimentality about the "life-balancing synergies in your child's journey to hope..."; mindless "on the one hand...but on the other" equivocation; inane advice that "you need to contact your school officials and health care providers"; and lazy instructions to "find an online tool." You don't want or need ambiguity or evasion. You want it straight and you'll get it straight.

This book is compact and to the point and as noted, I'm a loose and unfiltered guy. Some parts you will find difficult, even agonizing to read, other parts are easy going and light. This isn't going to be a march of despair.

The format

Uncomplicated author equals uncomplicated book.

First, to clarify: I'll use the word "lockdowns" as an overarching term for a range of pandemic-related actions: School, playground and park closures and the suspension of pre-pandemic kid social activity; the shuttering of malls, museums, movie theaters, sports activities; the quarantines, home confinement, the masking, the social distancing, the testing, the cancellation of signature events such as proms, weddings, summer jobs and summer camps and visits with loved ones. That's right, all of the pervasive anxiety and fear of the virus that sometimes verged on hysteria. *ALL* contributed to the unparalleled upset in the routines of children for which the costs are only now being calculated.

Second, I have focused on three basic areas in which the lockdown damage to youths was most acute - and yes, damage is a powerful word and it's relevant here. The chapters beyond directly address those areas and provide detailed advice that will help you:

Reverse your kid's increased use of screens and digital media
Restore your kid's confidence and mental well-being
Re-establish your kid's physical health and fitness

Each chapter leads with:

Stats and Facts — a section containing clinical and survey data providing a factual, empirical explanation of the effects of lockdowns on children and adolescents. The footnotes (and Appendixes to a full extent) provide cites to research by medical doctors, psychologists, educators, counselors, professional associations and national survey firms.

Then…

Rebound - a section containing the detailed series of steps you as a parent can take to incrementally reverse the bad habits that lockdowns either began or exacerbated in your child.

The key to the Rebound (as it was with *Four Lessons*) is serious and sustained parental engagement. Of course, this is not an original concept; it's a fundamental concept. It's the starting point for any change and this engagement succeeds in two ways:

1. It sets a permanent tone and gravity.

2. It is essential for kid buy-in.

The tone and the buy-in begins - the entire Rebound enterprise begins - with a Family Meeting at which is presented a Plan to be hammered out with your kids and then pursued relentlessly.

Family meetings clearly and unequivocally demonstrate a sense of solemnity and determination and purpose. The meetings set forth an ensuing family routine and the gatherings become a routine themselves. Getting your kids together to sit and talk is the most basic form of communication in a world full of communication channels. And the only truly valuable one.

If your family is not familiar with this type of practice or has eschewed them for one reason or another, then I would good-naturedly plead with you to undertake this step. After all, by reading this book you've already signaled you're ready for change.

The Meetings and the Plan outlined in each following chapter represent a *turning point* and depend totally on adherence. The *turnaround* will only begin when you make clear to your kids that certain facets of life are going to be different and that not following through is not an option. Without this structure, the kids – and you – will drift back to a daily life that is often disorganized, frustrating and....just like the past two years. Yes, think about that for a moment.

On a personal note, I will note that my family had these meetings throughout the childhood and adolescent years of my sons. We had the easy conversations and the tough conversations but there were fewer of the latter. Guess why.

AND FINALLY...

Checks. Throughout the book you'll see instances of sections preceded by a stylistic device: Reality Check, Gut Check, Echo Check, Nellie Check (the given Nelligan nickname for four generations). This means that something is so important to grasp that I can't help myself and in signature *Echo Check* fashion, I'll point it out again.

YOUR WAY FORWARD

This is a short, easy book to read, not a 300-page coffee table brick full of tortured psychobabble and generalizations. I hope it goads you into realizing that resignation to the aftermath of lockdowns is not an option.

Hyperbole Check: Your kid's Rebound – your family's Rebound – may be one of the most important endeavors you will ever undertake. If you're not sold, again, quicky think back to all the madness and frustration of the past two years.

Better yet, get real: Take a long, close look at your kid right this moment, with the insight and love only a parent possesses. Now. Imagine what he or she will be like and look like in one year, two years, five years if none of the lockdown acquired habits are changed.

Your way forward is found in the instructions herein. Revise them to fit your situation and then it's just simple, grinding tenacity. You'll not only get your kid back to where they were mentally, socially and physically, you will get them beyond.

CHAPTER 1

HOW YOU CAN REVERSE YOUR CHILD'S SCREEN USAGE AND OBSESSION

"Social media is training us to compare our lives instead of appreciating everything we are. No wonder why everyone is so depressed." Bill Murray

---

P *op Quiz*: How much time do you think teenagers spend on devices viewing digital media on an average day?

1. 5 hours 41 minutes

2. 4 hours 55 minutes

3. 7 hours

Answer: 8 Hours 39 minutes.

Surprised? Stunned? Consider very closely that sheer amount of time against all the activities of a 24-hour day – including school and interactions with family and friends. And sleep.

Oh, and guess what: That 8 hours 39 minutes is in addition to screen time spent on schoolwork. (1)

Now look in the mirror. The average American adult spends… wait for it…a total of 13 hours a day on some type of a screen (phone, iPad, and laptop). (2)

This screen-fest is not just isolated among teens and pre-teens. Preschoolers *under five years of age* with their own smartphones or tablets averaged two hours of screen time a day.

According to pediatric doctors writing in the *Journal of the American Medical Association* (JAMA), the more kids use screens in infancy, the more they'll use screens as they get older. "Children's average daily time spent watching television or using a computer or mobile device increased from 53 minutes at age 12 months to more than 150 minutes at 3 years," the study says. Contemplate this future: A brave new world featuring the Keystroke Kids. (3)

Reality Check: Does any reasonable parent think this amount of screen time among youths is healthy?

The singular feature of youthful lives in the decade prior to the Covid-19 pandemic was the time spent staring at phones, iPads, laptops, computers and gaming consoles, the devices from which pours forth torrents of the character-building content found on TikTok, Instagram, YouTube, SnapChat, Blendr, Kik, Fortnite, Ask.fm, Holla, Whisper, Call of Duty, Omegle, Facebook, Tumblr, Reddit, Pinterest, MeWe, and Minecraft to name just a handful of edifying platforms.

In fact, this staggering amount of screen time – precious hours spent gazing at what I call the "glowing rectangle' – can be harmful verging on devastating. First up the numbers. Then the consequences.

STATS AND FACTS

First, "obsession" with devices is not hyperbole. (4)

Prior to the pandemic daily screen viewing among tweens ages 8 to 12 was four hours and 44 minutes and among teens ages 13 to 18 it was seven hours and 22 minutes for teens. Now, as noted, the numbers are 8 hours 39 minutes. *That's approximately half the waking hours in a day.*

The numbers for kids under five years of age are equally alarming because they signal the beginning of a trend, as the *JAMA* study notes. A CommonSense Media survey of parents with a child under five revealed that that 51% of those kids used a tablet in 2020; it was 69% in 2021. For the same cohort, the number using a gaming device went from 16% to 29%. (5)

"In order for the brain's neural networks to develop normally during this critical period, a child needs specific stimuli from the outside environment. These are rules that have evolved over centuries of human evolution, but—not surprisingly—these essential stimuli are not found on today's tablet screens. When a young child spends too much time in front of a screen and not enough getting required stimuli from the real world, her development becomes stunted." Dr. Liraz Margalit, "Boundaries, Routines and Early Bedtimes: 13 Habits That Raise Well-Adjusted Kids," *Psychology Today*, April 16, 2016. (6)

THE DARK SIDE OF THE GLOWING RECTANGLE

What is the cost to a young person of these lost hours staring mutely at a screen?

Here we'll focus on the most prominent form of digital media, social media, where the effects of such prolonged viewing have been studied for nearly two decades by Dr. Jean Twenge and Dr. Jonathan Haidt, the nation's preeminent social media researchers.

They are unflinching: "Social media is strongly linked to unhappiness, especially for girls, with nearly each hour of use marching toward more unhappiness. Heavy users are almost twice as likely to be unhappy as light users. For boys there is little link to unhappiness until three to five hours a day while for girls the uptick in unhappiness appears after an hour of social media use a day."

More from Dr. Twenge:

"Most social media involves communicating with a group and not in real time. That gives it a performative aspect, with teens worrying about how many likes their posts will get and how many followers they have." Platforms such as Instagram "...have algorithms that expose teens to questionable content (such as pages encouraging unhealthy eating). In September 2021, internal company research leaked by a whistleblower showed that Instagram caused depression and body image issues among teen girls, causing in some cases a "grief spiral" of negative feelings. Instagram is, at base, a platform where teen girls and young women post pictures of their bodies and ask others to comment on them — not a good situation. In addition, as Instagram has grown in during the last decade, it has had particularly strong effects on girls and young women, inviting them to 'compare and despair' as they scrolled through posts from friends and strangers showing faces, bodies and lives that had been edited and re-edited until many were closer to perfection than to reality." (7)

"It's A Smartphone Life: Just over half of children in the United States — 53 percent — now own a smartphone by the age of 11. And 84 percent of teenagers now have their own phones." October 30, 2019, *National Public Radio.*

Cumulatively, the research of Drs. Twenge and Haidt shows that "rates of teenage depression, loneliness, self-harm and suicide began to rise sharply with widespread use of smartphones in 2010." In an August 2021 *New York Times* commentary, the pair wrote: "While there are likely a number of factors contributing to this [pandemic lockdown period] spike in suicide and mental health disorders, experts have specifically pointed to a relationship between excessive screen time – a problem that has existed for years but was drastically worsened during the pandemic – and health deterioration."

Bingo. One aspect of that deterioration is physical. Multiple studies have shown that extended screen time is directly correlated to obesity in young people and that obesity often leads to other serious mental and physical health issues, including further weight gain and binge eating. Dr. Jason Nagata, lead author on a *JAMA* pediatrics study brings science to the obvious: "Screen time lends itself to more sedentary time and less physical activity, snacking while distracted, eating in the absence of hunger, and greater exposure to food advertising." (8)

A subworld (yes, a fitting term) of the screen panorama involves video gaming.

According to a recent poll from the C.S. Mott Children's Hospital at the University of Michigan, adolescent boys are spending approximately three hours a day playing video games. *Nine in 10* parents surveyed said that their children were spending so much time gaming that their daily and family interactions were affected; that gaming is interfering with sleep in 46 percent of cases, with social interactions in 44 percent of cases, with friendships with peers who are not gaming with them by 33 percent, with homework in 34 percent and with extracurricular activities in 31 percent of cases. And, compared with non-gamers, adolescent gamers spent 30% less time reading and 34% less time doing homework. (9)

Let me give it to you hard and fast: As the stats above indicate, virtually every aspect of a gamer's school, social and family life - the central elements of a normal adolescence - is being obliterated by gaming. (10) (The good news: Junior is so skilled at Fortnite that he was the 7th player left standing in his last session of Battle Royale.)

Piling on....

- 50 percent of teens feel "addicted" to their phones. *Common Sense Media, 2016*

- 59 percent of U.S teens have been bullied or harassed online. *Pew Research Center, 2018*

- 39 percent of teens have sent or posted sexually suggestive messages (sexting). *GuardChild 2017*

- Technology is making children dangerously unhealthy. *World Health Organization, 2017*

From *Raising Humans in a Digital World: Helping Kids Build a Healthy Relationship with Technology by* Diana Graber, HarperCollins Leadership, January 2019

Another key point Dr. Twenge and many others have raised repeatedly: Any child under 13 *should not be on these platforms.* The Children's Online Privacy Protection Act of 1998 (COPPA; 15 U.S.C. 6501–6505) decrees that under-13 kids are not allowed to have a social media page in their own name. As Dr. Twenge notes, "some kids will lie about their age and once that happens, other kids don't want to be excluded, so they feel pressured to do the same." Moreover, "the age minimum is unevenly enforced by the platforms. Even 13 is likely too young as it comes during the fraught years of middle school when social pressures are already running high." (Additional information on COPPA is found in Appendix B.)

Dr. Twenge brings it home: "Light users of digital media reported substantially higher psychological well-being than heavy users; heavy users (vs. light) of digital media were 48% to 171% more likely to be unhappy, to be low in well-being, or to have suicide risk factors such as depression, suicidal ideation, or past suicide attempts. Heavy users (vs. light) were twice as likely to report having attempted suicide. Light users (rather than non- or moderate users) were highest in well-being."

NELLIE TALE

I got a very early wakeup call on the absolute power and grip of the glowing rectangle and as you can obviously see from the thunder above, it has colored my thinking on the matter ever since.

Like most parents of young children, our family bought familiar, kid-oriented DVDs - Clifford the Big Red Dog, Dragon Tales, Redwall, and Scooby Doo - figuring it would be fun entertainment. The eldest was five years of age at the time, the others four and one. We'd watch them in the evening several times a week and indeed it was enjoyable and the boys were delighted.

After about six or seven months of this routine, I began noticing something a bit eerie: The boys were gradually becoming transfixed by the whole experience. When one video ended they would beg to watch another, then another. Then, there came the constant pleas throughout the day to watch a video that night. Normally energetic and care-free, they became utterly different kids when the screen was on, frozen in a near catatonic state. The whole cycle was exactly the same with watching television programs. The pleading for more, the badgering throughout the day, the zombie-style attention and then petulance and anger when the television was shut off.

After about eight months of this craziness I'd had enough and told them so: 'Boys, we're going to make some changes and you're not going to like them.'

Here's where we visit and will revisit down the line a basic fact: I am the parent. My three sons are kids. I am in charge. Or to put the counterintuitive twist on a phrase the eldest sometimes used when unhappy: 'Yes, *I am* the boss of you.'

We then did what needed to be done: We had a family meeting to air it all out and we developed a plan. It wasn't a funfest but we had to set the edge on the entire video-television scene. And here were the rules:

1. No more kid videos. Period. I told them instead we'd buy all the *Magic Tree House* and *Boxcar Children* editions and read them out loud (we ultimately got up to #37, *Dragon of the Red Dawn* in the former, and #97, *The Radio Mystery* in the latter).

2. Television viewing would be limited to sporting events and old-school style programming, which meant from the ages of six onwards my sons watched, with a parent in attendance, such masterpieces as *South Pacific, West Side Story, Annie Get Your Gun, The Apple Dumpling Gang, Mary Poppins, The Wizard of Oz, Oklahoma* and many other classics from the way back machine.

3. Let me anticipate and answer what you might be wondering: Yes, kids will get into these types of shows if it's the only game in town. Adjustments were made along the way for sure. We'd watch signature national events being aired and sometimes break down and watch a network program.

Enforcing these policies as the years rolled on, we hung tough on the purchase and use of digital devices.

1. When the eldest was 12, each kid was allowed one hour of video gaming. A week.

2. Of course they were allowed to use the home computer for schoolwork and later, the school-required iPad. But they were on an honor system with regards to extensive use of the internet not related to said schoolwork.

3. They didn't receive iPhones until each entered 11th grade. And another Nellie gambit: At the end of each day, I'd give a dollar to the kid who had the most battery power left on their phone.

And yes, I know what you're thinking because at the time I thought of it as well: Whenever they were not at home — i.e., at their friends' houses - they had access to screens.

They knew full well my concerns about the "interweb" - our jokey term for all things screens - and I'd say to them from time to time, "Hey guys, I can't stop you from watching stuff but do me a favor and don't go overboard. I trust you on this." And I did.

Now, with all of this background comes the set up for your kid's....

REBOUND

The goal is to gradually reverse your child's infatuation with screens and all digital media. Of course, after reading the statistics and commentary above (the vulnerability of your daughter, your son's descent into fantasy worlds) some parents might want to immediately rip the devices right out of their kids' hands. You can only do that with very young kids because yes, you are the boss of them. Tweens and teens can rebel – and you know this well - in ways unavailable to younger children.

First up: The guidance and suggestions below have been assembled from a wide range of psychologists, medical professionals, counselors, technical experts (i.e., web experts) and yes, parents who've simply had enough.

The chief sources below are our friends Dr. Twenge and Dr. Haidt, to which I will add Dr. Devorah Heitner and Diana Graber (further background on all four is found in Appendix B).

Their recommendations are targeted at three areas:

1. Vastly limiting the use of digital media in your kid's life;

2. Protecting him or her from the unsavory aspects of the world wide web, including predators; and,

3. Providing you specific information on how to technically manage, through (where else?!) online platforms, what your kids can and cannot see.

Applying yourself forcefully to the three areas above will require you to establish boundaries and devote yourself to follow-through action that sometimes is easy and sometimes is difficult. But get real: You're the parent and you're in charge.

"The most effective vehicle for improving children's outcomes is not the school or the church or even the job center; it is the family—or, if necessary, the creation of substitute or supplemental family structures for children who don't have them." Paul Tough, *How Children Succeed: Grit, Curiosity, and the Hidden Power of Character, New York Times Bestseller, Mariner Press.*

Moreover, given your family dynamics, you may eschew or modify parts of these recommendations. As with all the suggestions in this book, the steps should be incremental and the only time to start *is now*.

THE FAMILY MEETING AND THE PLAN

Reality Check: Recall my words on Family Meetings in Chapter 1!

1. Arrange a family meeting and make it clear that it's not going to be brief. In fact, it will last as long as it has to.

There will be no interruptions, no distractions, and there will be absolutely no electronic devices in the room or within earshot. This alone plays the drama card and will arouse their curiosity. This is going to be a discussion of consequence. Paper and pens required for all.

2. Begin the discussion with your concerns about your kid or kids' screen habits and *use the quiz at the top of this chapter.* Quote some of the other numbers cited regarding digital media and its dangers. Come clean on your own use of screens.

3. Then engage your kid or kids with questions: Diana Graber, author of *Raising Humans in a Digital World: Helping Kids Build a Healthy Relationship with Technology* suggests a great starting point: Ask your kid or kids to analyze how they spend their time on their phones and computers over the course of a single day. Then, ask them to create, right now, a list of 5 things they would do if screens didn't exist. Call it the Wish List. Make your own list and show it to them.

4. Now, announce that the family is going to take a one-day hiatus from screen usage not affiliated with school-work and your professional work and that each family member is going to begin one of the five things on their Wish List.

5. Announce that the next meeting is in 24 hours.

If this all this sounds elementary or unsophisticated, good. That means it won't be hard for you. Keep going.

6. At the next meeting you air it out. How did everyone feel for those 24-hours? What did they do with the time? Tell them what you did with your time.

7. Repeat 24 hours later. After more discussion about digital media and devices and the content watched, you then announce that the family is going to draft and sign a ***Screen Contract.*** There are three samples in Appendix A.

FASHIONING THE SCREEN CONTRACT FOR YOUR FAMILY

Print out the Contracts (links provided in Appendix A) and either decide upon one or mix the elements within each.

As you discuss the Contract some of the items below might factor into your discussion. These are suggestions only and might give you and your kids further ideas on how you collectively are going to manage – *and limit* - screen time and digital media use going forward.

Consider...

• No phones at school. That's right, you send them off phoneless. Dr. Twenge notes that this forces "students

[to] practice the lost art of paying full attention to the people around them — including their teachers."

- Detail when and where kids can use the various types of devices and content and for how long. Ms. Graber suggests: Younger kids can watch YouTube only when a parent is in the room with them.

- No screens past a certain time. This is huge. Again, Dr. Twenge: "Eliminate screens in the hour before bedtime. Digital activities are both psychologically stimulating (Did my crush text me back? Did anyone like my Instagram post?) and physiologically stimulating (the blue light from devices tricks our brains into thinking it's still daytime). When phones and tablets are within reach during sleep time, sleep quality and length both suffer."

- And this one is simple: Inform the teen that the already limited phone usage could be shut off if their grades drop.

You have all you need – design and sign that contract!

THE MORE TROUBLING DANGERS THAN SCREEN TIME

There are two remaining areas where a discussion with kids is absolutely required:

1. Online predators; and,

2. Privacy concerns.

Both subjects form the most alarming part of this book. If you read nothing else, read these sections. Twice.

PREDATORS

Here's simple and chilling language from The Beau Biden Foundation:

"The Internet and social media platforms have kicked the doors wide open for child predators to hunt, lure, and groom victims online. Every day there are at least 500,000 predators online. One in five children report they've been solicited or contacted by a predator in the last year. Oftentimes children inadvertently fall into the traps set by predators. 46% of children give information away about themselves online – perfect tools for predators to use to identify victims, build trust and establish relationships around shared interests." (10)

Frightening for sure and there's more:

"Children between the ages of 12 and 15 are especially susceptible to be groomed or manipulated by adults they meet online. According to the F.B.I., over 50 percent of the victims of online sexual exploitation are between the ages of 12 and 15. An estimated 89 percent of sexual advances directed at children occur in Internet chatrooms or through instant messaging. In over a

quarter of all reported exploitation incidents, the online predator will ask a child for sexually explicit photos of themselves."

Here's how it starts:

"A predator targets a child in a public chat, on a social media
platform or in an online game. The predator may comment
on a social media post or send a direct message. To gain trust,
predators will typically lie about their age – they may adopt a
persona that's just a bit older than the potential victim.

Predators then take the conversation further by asking more
private questions, often in a different, more secretive app [see
"Apps within Apps" section below] to test the child's boundaries. Questions turn more personal, as they ask about other
relationships the child has – with parents, friends, teachers,
other adults. Predators use this information to build walls between a child and peers in their lives to further isolate them.

Conversations start innocently enough, and a predator may
offer small tokens of appreciation, praise, or a willingness to
listen at any hour. As the connection develops over time, the
predator will offer the child small gifts – in the case of online
gaming, the resources or currency used in the game. Perhaps
it's a gift card or something seemingly innocent the child may
not be able to purchase themselves." (Additional information
found in Appendix B).

Gut Check: Do you find the above as terrifying as I do?!
It's why you must have a frank discussion with your kids about online predators.

Pop Quiz II: Do you know what apps your kids have on their phones?

Ask them. And I *guarantee* they'll answer with most or even all of following: WhatsApp, Instagram, Skype, Facebook Messenger, Musical.ly, Twitter, Group Play, Pinterest, Snapchat, TikTok, and YouTube. These are the most popular apps used by adolescents. (12)

But there will be others. Ask your child about the following apps, whose names alone should make a parent shudder:

HouseParty, Hoop, Discord, Kik, Holla, Chatspin, Pericsope, kout, Badoo, Hot or Not, Omegle, Kik, Ask.fm, Whisper, AfterSchool, GroupMe, Blendr, Doublicat, VSCO, MeetMe, Oooh.me, Tinder, Grindr, Yik Yak, Keek, Chatroulette, Chat-Avenue, ChatStep, Chatrandom, Camzap, Tinychat, Tohlam, Skout, Badoo...yeah, the list goes on and on and on.

Get this straight: Did you know that most of these apps in one form or another...

1. Allow random strangers – in your community, your state and worldwide - to follow your kids' profile and share photos, videos and audio?

2. That there is always the ever-present danger that these apps reveal to your child outrageous, vile, and vulgar content?.

Below are brief details on just eight of the apps named above, drawn from experts at the cyber-security firm *fenced.ai*

"*Omegle* is a free chat and video communication platform that lets two parties communicate without creating an account. The service randomly pairs two people with names assigned "You", creating a session for communication.

Kik is similar to *Omegle*; no accounts, random strangers, and it's well-known for cyberbullying.

Ask.fm and *Oooh.me* are platforms where anonymous users can ask questions – yes, accelerating from innocuous to vulgar to entrapping - and other people answer those questions. There is also no online moderator and adult profiles are mixed in with those of teens and children. Users can also write the questions and the answers anonymously.

Whisper is an app where people write their confessions anonymously; unfortunately, many teens use this app. It also uses a GPS tracker meaning that although the identity of the user may be anonymous, predators can locate any user.

Blendr is a flirting app that shows nearby users interested in talking to strangers and being flirty; wide-open to theft of a user's personal information.

4chan is similar to Reddit in that it is a large user-run forum but it is known for being subversive and offensive. Many topics are inappropriate for kids and teens.

And then there are what is known as *Pro-Ana Websites* - websites devoted to promoting anorexia and sometimes bulimia. These websites typically have "tips" for how to starve yourself and prevent hunger. The forums also allow individuals to post anonymous comments and compare the progression of their weight loss." (13)

<u>Get this in your head</u>: The material above is a brief overview of just a handful of apps and platforms available to your kid every single time he or she is on a phone, iPad or laptop. Are you as a parent comfortable with your kid's presence on any of these sites?! With his or her personal information being available to strangers in your zip code or the next town or state?! And here's the toughest question of all: Do you trust your kid to immediately exit out and turn away from the sudden images of violent and adult material that appears on these platforms?

ALAS, MORE BAD NEWS: APPS WITHIN APPS

Equally creepy are the *apps that hide apps* (as if the cyberverse couldn't get more twisted). These apps are designed to hide apps and platforms and attendant caches of photos, videos and messages. Why?

Unfortunately, kids want to hide what they're doing from Mom and Dad. Yes, imagine that.

Here are some: Hide It Pro, Private Photo Vault, KeepSafe, Secret Calculator Vault, FotoX, Photo Locker, AppLock Private Photo, and KYMS. All feature innocuous icons on a phone screen - some a calendar, some a calculator — that hide vast amounts of kid information. (14) And yes, I'll say it: Check their phones for these apps.

You and I know that the world - both real and cyber - is full of shadows and within those shadows are legions of perverted individuals; the world wide web has only expanded their reach.

TAKE CHARGE: HERE'S WHAT YOU CAN DO...
From The Beau Biden Foundation website is a simple but valuable list of precautions you can take to protect your child:

- "Pay attention to items your child may have that you did not provide, such as a mobile phone, gift cards, or clothing;

- Ask yourself if your child is being secretive about online activity;

- Talk to your child about online predators in the same way your parents talked to you about "stranger danger" – but be specific;

- Talk to your child about what they're sharing online. Help them understand how personal information can be used by predators to begin a conversation or establish trust;

- Talk to your child about how to shut down a conversation with someone they suspect is a predator. For example, if your child is asked for their home address, suggest they respond with the address of a local police station;

- Monitor your child's device. Know what apps they're using, and the chat functions those apps have built into them; and,

- Read their chats."

PRIVACY

Here is the second serious discussion you should have with your kid. The tips below are drawn from Elana Pearl Ben-Joseph, MD, of Nemours Health. Once again, perhaps they sound elementary. Good. They should be easy to convey to your child. Do so with conviction.

- "Never post or trade personal pictures;

- Never reveal personal information, such as address, phone number, or school name or location;

- Use only a screen name and don't share passwords (other than with parents);

- Never agree to get together in person with anyone met online without parent approval and/or supervision;

- Never respond to a threatening email, message, post, or text; and,

- Always tell Mom or Dad about any communication or conversation that was frightening or hurtful." (15)

WALK THE WALK

As you set the new parameters of screen and digital media usage for your kids, you must change your habits as well. Your modeling of good behavior is a key part of the move towards a reduced-screen world. I know. Because in humiliating fashion I learned the hard way.

NELLIE TALE

When my kids were pre-teens I had a political job in which I was in touch with all types of individuals during all hours of the day and night. As you know yourself, this is how the professional world works. At one point about eight months into the job I was shooting hoops in the front yard with the boys when my phone buzzed. Automatically I pivoted to look at the device and suddenly my middle kid gives this big sigh and says to me in frustration, "Dad, why are you always on your phone?" Oh man, major league call-out. There I was, a warrior against screens and the Interweb and bang, here's my son with the blinding truth about my hypocrisy. It made me sick. Worse, it suddenly hit me that up to this moment my sons had seen me time and again turn away from them to focus on my phone. It was one of the starkest moments of shame and disgust I've ever had as a parent. I told him he was right and I was wrong and that I'm glad he'd said something.

I vowed to change. In fact, I was so floored by that encounter in the driveway that during the next *ten years* I may have yanked my phone out a dozen times in their presence. If the email or call was really important, I waited until I could separate myself from a son or sons – 'Give me five, guys' I'd say – and then deal with it. Even thinking and writing about this incident today makes me wince. And it should.

The next step: Parental control of apps and platforms

You may think *control* is a loaded word. But maybe not so loaded as you absorb what you've read above about inordinate screen usage time, psychological impairments, the questionable content on everyday apps and platforms and a Web alive with predators.

"Severe moderation of screens can be difficult for teens themselves to implement," write Drs. Twenge and Haidt. "The algorithms of social media sites are designed to be addictive, keeping users on the site as long as possible. Thus, it's probably a good idea to use the parental controls available on most devices to limit the amount of time your teen spends on social media apps." Bingo once more.

Certainly, the Screen Contract and family discussions will yield promises and inducements and warnings. Nevertheless, there are failsafe ways to monitor and manage the tidal wave of digital media and below is a good list of the most popular services that do just that. Even if you don't think parental controls are right for you or your family, humor me and just read the next few paragraphs.

Brad Stephenson is an editor and writer for the Microsoft Technology News Site (MFST) and a great source on parental control apps and services, about which he writes: "These products can limit screen time and phone usage while also filtering the types of websites your child can access when surfing the web. They are variously available on iOS, Android, Windows, Mac, and Kindle. Some are free; some have a nominal monthly charge, reasonable enough. What they do:

- Control the apps their child downloads on their mobile phone;

- Allot how much screen time they're allowed each day and the content they can purchase;

- Track the location of the child's phone, monitor web and app usage, and record call numbers;

- Place time limits on video games;

- Block specific apps; and,

- Record Skype chats."

And here they are:

Google Family Link, KidLogger, Qustodio, Bark, Nintendo Switch Parental Controls, Microsoft Family Safety, PlayStation Gamers: Family on PSN, and OpenDNS FamilyShield." (16)

LEDGER LINE

You perhaps began this chapter ambivalent about your kid's devices and the vast panorama of the digital universe.

Maybe now you feel a bit different. Maybe you're not comfortable with the amount of time screens suck out of your kid's day or what extreme usage leads to. Perhaps you weren't familiar with the details of some of the apps on your kid's phone. Or with the extent of compromise these apps contain. Or with the dynamics of how predators operate and ensnare.

Check back to the pop quiz at the top: Average cell phone use at 8 hours and 49 minutes a day during pandemic lockdowns. More time than spent at school. More time than spent sleeping. More time than spent with the family. ot to play the drama card but...

During that nearly nine hours, what opportunities were missed with schooling, with activities, with friends, with you? What conversations never happened, what good-natured horsing around with friends never occurred? What did nearly nine hours of mute gazing do for your kid?!

You now have the facts, you now know the questionable extremities of the digital world. You have a lengthy list of specific, commonsensical, doable actions you can take to reverse the negative habits — and their consequences - documented above.

I don't even have to tell you that to reverse this tide you'll encounter a scene and sullen or angry pushback. After nearly two years social distancing, contagion fears, remote schooling and increased reliance on devices, your kids are not going spontaneously and happily ease up on their glowing rectangle use.

That's why you'll have to go on offense with regular discussions with your kids and the screen contract. I guarantee you will make progress. Prove to your kids that you are not going away on this issue. Begin to break the screen stranglehold and get your kid back.

Footnotes

1. "The Common Sense Census: Media Use by Tweens and Teens," Editors, CommonSenseMedia.org, March 9, 2022. https://www.commonsensemedia.org/research/the-common-sense-census-media-use-by-tweens-and-teens-2021

2. "2022 Cell Phone Usage Statistics: How Obsessed Are We?" By Trevor Wheelwright, Reviews.org, January 24, 2022. On average, Americans check their phones 344 times per day. 71% of us check our phones within 10 minutes of waking up; 74% of us can't leave our cell phones at home without feeling uneasy; 48% of people say they feel a sense of panic or anxiety when their cell phone battery goes below 20%. Even while driving, 35% of Americans use or look at their cell phones. https://www.reviews.org/mobile/cell-phone-addiction/#:~:text=How%20often%20are%20we%20using,phones%20are%20our%20constant%20companions

3. JAMA cite from footnote 1. https://jamanetwork.com/journals/jamapediatrics/fullarticle/2792736#:~:text=Some%20evidence%20suggests%20that%20some,concerns%20should%20also%20be%20

4. JAMA Pediatrics Patient Page, May 31, 2022, "Social Media Use in Children and Adolescents," by Meryl Shychuk, MD; Nancy Joseph, MD; Lindsay A. Thompson, MD. https://jamanetwork.com/journals/jamapediatrics/fullarticle/2792736#:~:text=Some%20evidence%20suggests%20that%20some,concerns%20should%20also%20be%20

5. "The Common Sense Census: Media Use by Tweens and Teens," Editors, CommonSenseMedia.org, March 9, 2022. https://www.commonsensemedia.org/research/the-common-sense-census-media-use-by-tweens-and-teens-2021

6. "What Screen Time Can Really Do to Kids' Brains: Too much at the worst possible age may have negative consequences" by Dr. Liz Marlit, *Psychology Today*, April 16, 2016. https://www.psychologytoday.com/us/blog/behind-online-behavior/201604/what-screen-time-can-really-do-kids-brains

7. My fave duo: "This Is Our Chance to Pull Teenagers Out of the Smartphone Trap," New York Times, July 31, 2021,by Dr. Jean Twenge and Dr. Jonathan Haidt. https://www.nytimes.com/2021/07/31/opinion/smartphone-iphone-social-media-isolation.htmll In addition: "Dr. Twenge discovered that 2012 was the first year that a majority of Americans owned a smartphone; by 2015, two-thirds of teens

did too. This was also the period when social media use moved from optional to ubiquitous among adolescents. Dr. Haidt learned, while writing an essay with the technologist Tobias Rose-Stockwell, that the major social media platforms changed profoundly from 2009 to 2012. In 2009, Facebook added the like button, Twitter added the retweet button and, over the next few years, users' feeds became algorithmicized based on "engagement," which mostly meant a post's ability to trigger emotions." Guess what kind. More: "The evidence is not just circumstantial; we also have eyewitness testimony. In 2017, British researchers asked 1,500 teens to rate how each of the major social-media platforms affected them on certain well-being measures, including anxiety, loneliness, body image, and sleep. Instagram scored as the most harmful, followed by Snapchat and then Facebook The victims point to Instagram. Far easier to show is the damage to a specific class of people: adolescent girls, whose rates of depression, anxiety, and self-injury surged in the early 2010s, as social-media platforms proliferated and expanded. By 2019, just before the pandemic, rates of depression among adolescents had nearly doubled from 2012."

8. "Screen Time Increases Teenagers' Incidence of Overweight and Obesity," by PW Staff, Jul 20, 2022, *Physician's Weekly* and the *Department of the Obvious.* https://www.physiciansweekly.com/

screen-time-increases-teenagers-incidence-of-over-weight-and-obesity

9. "Adolescents' recreational screen time doubled during pandemic, affecting mental health," University of California at San Francisco Department of Epidemiology and Biostatistics, November 21, 2021 https://epibiostat.ucsf.edu/news/adolescents%E2%80%99-recreational-screen-time-doubled-during-pandemic-affecting-mental-health

10. "What should I know about video games and kids?" Editors, Boston Children's Hospital, https://digitalwellnesslab.org/parents/video-games/

11. "How do predators find children online?" Editors, The Beau Biden Foundation for the Protection of Children, June 2021. https://www.beaubidenfoundation.org/onlinepredatorsblog1/

12. "18 Most Dangerous Social Media Apps," Staff, fenced.ai, February 2022. https://fenced.ai/blogs/18-most-dangerous-social-media-apps/

13. "Secret Vault Apps That Hide Things on Your Kid's Phone," Editors, *NetNanny.com*, July 2020. Yes, it's come to this: The apps that hide apps - https://www.netnanny.com/blog/secret-vault-apps-that-hide-things-on-your-kid-e2-80-99s-phone/

14. "Online Safety" by Elana Pearl Ben-Joseph, MD, Nemours Health, August 2022. Good information all around. https://kidshealth.org/en/parents/net-safety.html Also useful: "Internet safety for children 6-8 years," Editors, raisingChildren. net.au, May 2022 https://raisingchildren.net.au/ school-age/play-media-technology/online-safety/ internet-safety-6-8-years

15. "The 10 Best Parental Control Apps and Services of 2022 / Apps and services for everything from limiting screen time to tracking locations," by Brad Stephenson, Lifewire.com, July 18, 2022. The most extensive and useful piece on parental controls. https://www.lifewire.com/ best-parental-control-apps-4691864

CHAPTER 2

How you can restore your kid's Confidence and Mental Well-Being

---

"Do the one thing you think you cannot do. Fail at it. Try again. Do better the second time. The only people who never tumble are those who never mount the high wire." Oprah Winfrey

---

As noted in the Preface, I wrote a book about helping raise my three sons from childhood through adolescence and beyond. The technique I used to develop my sons' personal conduct and character relied upon comedic observations about people and situations in everyday life, a rather colorful landscape with which all parents are familiar. (1)

My light touch led to hard lessons about how the boys should handle themselves in that relentless real world in which we all live. My chief goal was to develop a resilient kid who when encountering adversity would reflexively not retreat but drive forward with resolve. And by adversity, I mean the unforeseen setbacks - academic failings, friction with peers, disagreements with parents, family economic challenges, abrupt situations with strangers, public embarrassments – that you and I have encountered with our children. These are some of the common challenges faced by every young person and every parent has been a witness.

HOWEVER,...

My book focused on distinct moments of adversity. Today's scene and saga is entirely different. Parents and their kids have lived through *nearly two years of adversity.*

I'll say it another way: Few could have contemplated the kind of across-the-board turmoil and hardship that kids would suffer from society-wide lockdowns. I said "few" because some individuals did in fact predict what would happen and their warnings went unheeded. (2)

Having spoken with hundreds of parents and kids during this time and having read everything I could get my hands on (thus the 200 cites) it's clear that the cumulative effect of lockdowns and an 18-month-long bunker mentality have had a severe effect on youth mental health, confidence, and self-esteem.

What is the only way to restore a child's self-assurance and poise and balance? Parental engagement. That is, a concentrated and sustained push from you in setting new patterns in your kid's daily family and social life.

First, we'll examine the psychological injuries of lockdowns and then dig in on the how restoration plays out.

STATS AND FACTS

From March 15th, 2020 onwards, American society undertook, with little supporting historical, clinical or epidemiological data or evidence, a profound experiment: The near-complete suspension of social and economic activity for which our purposes in this book the closures of schools was most prominent. This affected almost all kids, no matter their socio-economic background, race, and geographical location. (There were outliers – states including Georgia, Florida, Mississippi, Tennessee, Indiana, South Dakota, Texas opened schools in August of 2020). (3).

The broader extent of these lockdowns – pushed by Federal, state, and local authorities - was just not about schools. It included, as you know firsthand, the closure of youth sports and activities and jobs, childcare facilities, libraries, recreational centers, movie theaters, malls, playgrounds, parks, proms, and graduations (and again, you can no doubt add more to this list). The result was a near total suspension of personal, face-to-face contact with peers and the world at large.

What happened next?

As early as June 2020, researchers at the National Library of Medicine reported: "Early indications in the COVID-19 context indicate that more than one-third of adolescents report high levels of loneliness and almost half of 18 to 24-year olds are lonely during lockdown." As a post-lockdown paper published by the National Library of Medicine in 2022 notes, the links between loneliness and mental health are interlocked. (4)

Reality check: The June 2020 figures were compiled *just three months into the nationwide lockdowns.*

Six months into lockdowns, the American Academy of Pediatrics reported: "… the numbers paint an alarming picture. Between March and October 2020, the percentage of emergency department visits for children with mental health emergencies rose by 24 percent for children ages 5-11 and 31 percent for children ages 12-17."

Fourteen months into lockdowns, Amy Wimpey Knight, president of Children's Hospital Association (CHA) stated what a growing number of parents could see for themselves, "We are facing a significant national mental health crisis in our children and teens which requires urgent action. In the first six months of this year [2021], children's hospitals across the country reported a shocking 45 percent increase in the number of self-injury and suicide cases in 5- to 17-year-olds compared to the same period in 2019. There was also a more than 50 percent increase in suspected suicide attempt emergency department visits among girls ages 12-17 in early 2021 as compared to the same period in 2019." (5)

Some of the mental and behavioral health conditions in the CHA analysis include depressive disorders, anxiety disorders, stress disorders, eating disorders and suicidal ideation.

Health insurance payments company Clarify Health studied data covering 2016 through 2021 for mental health related insurance claims for children ages 1 to 19 with "very sharp increases starting in 2020. "By age groups, teenagers aged 12 to 15 and 16 to 19 fared worse than the younger age groups. Girls aged 12 to 15 had an 84 percent increase for inpatient admissions per 1,000 patients, and boys in the same age group saw an 83 percent increase. Emergency Department visits increased by 41 percent for girls and 38 percent for boys in this age group." (6)

And lockdowns didn't just affect American kids. A YouGov Children's Omnibus survey of 1,013 UK children between the ages of 6 and 15 in December of 2020 reported the COVID-19 pandemic and UK lockdowns resulted in an increase in negative emotions and at the same time a decrease in positive feelings. Over half (56%) of children reported feeling more worried compared to how they were before March of 2020. More than four in ten (42%) said they felt more trapped since March 2020; a further two in five (41%) felt more scared than they used to, with only 5% reporting feeling this way less than previously." (7)

Twenty-one months into lockdowns, an extensive report from *CBS News* was stark: "In 2022, fifteen percent of kids ages 12 to 17 reported experiencing at least one major depressive episode. That figure represents an increase of 306,000 cases from 2021, a trend line that is troubling health experts. Tragically, this rise in mental health conditions for American youth has also coincided with a sharp uptick in suicide and suicide attempts." (8) At the same time, the CDC reported that one in five American teenagers say they have contemplated suicide, while four in ten say they feel "persistently sad or hopeless." (9)

One last heartbreaker: Here's a CDC report summarized by USA Today: "A survey published Thursday (October 13, 2022) found a majority of high school students reported a potentially traumatic event during the COVID-19 pandemic that may have contributed to poor mental health and suicidal behaviors." Of course, there's a certain irony in an agency cataloging the damage of many of the policies developed and put in place by that agency. (10)

EDUCATIONAL LOSSES

The separation from classrooms and peers and school activities undeniably effected the mental and social well-being of young people. Now we know that separated from the pre-lockdown school environment, Zoom classes and online learning resulted in a catastrophic hit to the educational progress of children, pre-teens and adolescents kids.

How bad? As *The Wall Street Journal* observed in August of 2022: "The National Assessment of Educational Progress (NAEP) scores for 2022 are a calamity. An unprecedented decline in reading and math scores is the first national measure of the damage done by school closures to America's children."

More: "The 2020 NAEP tests were administered shortly before pandemic lockdowns and school closures, so this year's results provide a snapshot of how students have weathered those two years. It's not pretty. Average nine-year-old scores declined the most on record in math (seven points) and in reading since 1990 (five points). *Two decades of progress have been erased in two years"* [emphasis mine]. (11)

"Student health clinics and mental health professionals are inundated with young people suffering from pandemic school closures and the resulting social isolation and disruption to their lives. Did anybody expect average test scores to do anything but drop? Did we need them to tell us students aren't doing well?" Valerie Strauss, *Washington Post*, October 17, 2022.

Dr. Thomas Kane, the Director of the Center for Education Policy Research at Harvard University sums it up: "The [school] closures came at a stiff price—a large decline in children's achievement overall and a historic widening in achievement gaps by race and economic status. The achievement loss is far greater than most educators and parents seem to realize." (11 & 12)

Virtually every measure of childhood and adolescent life pursued with vigor in February of 2020 was upended.

41

Prolonged isolation from their peers and the social rhythms and routines of life were devastating. You know this and your anecdotal evidence is supported by undisputed facts.

Had enough? For all parents, this torrent of statistics is absolutely heart wrenching. For some it's not news. They've seen it firsthand.

Now, for children to regain that mental and social well-being and stability - to get back what I call the well-adjusted kid – will require new patterns of family life and it all begins with you.

REBOUND

Here's a change-up:

Think back to your kid's overall outlook and mood on January 1, 2020 when there was only the faintest whisper of virus loose in Wuhan, China. Thank back to his or her overall behavior and state of mind, awaking and starting the day with constancy and stability and feeling secure about themselves and their place in the home and school and the world around them. Now think about what your child is like now.

Behaviors different? Personality? Attitude? Their pursuits then being pursued now with the same energy and happiness and motivation?

Lauren Tamm, who runs the popular *Military Mom* website, has written something I treasure because it's just so elegantly simple: "Kids cannot even think at the maturity level needed to break a behavior cycle, let alone do anything about it. So, as the parents, it has to start with us." (13) It's worth repeating: The foundation for well-adjusted kids always starts with us.

Perhaps your kid is about the same today as he or she was on January 1, 2020. Then congratulations is in order with no facetiousness whatsoever. But if your kid is not same, keep reading. As trite and hackneyed and overused as it may seem, the fact is - as everyone from child psychologists to counselors to teachers to coaches and parents all agree— it all begins with getting a kid to believe in themselves. As Nemours Health experts write: "Kids who feel good about themselves have the confidence to try new things. They are more likely to try their best, cope with mistakes, and try again even if they fail at first." Maybe that sounds a lot like your kid before lockdown madness.

The converse, of course, is that "kids with low self-esteem or confidence are self-critical and hard on themselves, feel they're not as good as other kids, think of the times they fail rather than when they succeed. If they think others won't accept them, they may not join in. They may let others treat them poorly. Kids with low self-esteem find it hard to cope when they make a mistake, lose, or fail." (14) Maybe that sounds like your kid now.

"What matters most in a child's development, they say, is not how much information we can stuff into her brain in the first few years. What matters, instead, is whether we are able to help her develop a very different set of qualities, a list that includes persistence, self-control, curiosity, conscientiousness, grit and self-confidence." Paul Tough, *How Children Succeed: Grit, Curiosity, and the Hidden Power of Character*

Let me flail the obvious here: I've been around kids of all ages for more than two decades in every setting and situation known to the American parent. I have seen kids with solid self-esteem and those who lack of self-esteem. Each is easy to spot. We're not talking about a characteristic that is easily hidden. The self-esteem gap, alas, is in plain sight and the good news is that it can be closed. If it's not? Beware the fragile son or daughter.

Restoring the confidence and mental well-being damaged by lockdowns should be your goal. And like every goal in this book, it's best done incrementally.

THE FAMILY MEETING AND THE PLAN
I won't repeat what I wrote in Chapters 1 and 2.

Echo check: I will: I cannot emphasize the importance of both. The Meeting elevates the topic, it gets all the thoughts and feelings out there, it helps get buy-in from your kids. Over time, the Meeting itself becomes a routine bringing structure where there was perhaps little or none.

The Plan sets the path. From the voluminous information below (again, drawn from dozens of psychologists, counselors, teachers and parents) you can devise what will work for you and your family, cheery pick what you find useful.

Here's your entry into a new way of family functioning.

A SUGGESTED OPENER...

At the meeting, lay it out plainly: "We all know the pandemic upset each of us all as individuals and as a family. We are kind of getting back to normal and what it was like before. But I don't think what we had before was good enough and maybe you don't either. That's why we are all going to make changes that will make us better as individuals and as a family. Some changes will not be hard, some will be very hard. We've all lost a step or more and we're going to use this setback to get to a better place. And the first thing we're going to start with is..." Yes, I'll say it again – this meeting intro sounds elementary because it is. You may well have better ideas. Good. Use them.

ROUTINES

A simple concept with big payoffs: A predictable home environment with few surprises and few conflicts; where every kid and Mom and Dad knows their role, knows what will happen during a given day, week and month; where everyone knows the score and feels organized and in control; where there is little uncertainty and lots of structure, which helps a child become more independent and as a result, more confident.

Organization produces calm in the here and now and the future. I know from experience it's best not to dive into a lot of routines at once. Ease into one and lock it up and then ease into another. Routines take some effort to establish but you'll immediately see the benefits. (15)

MONTHLY CALENDAR

The Routine of all Routines is creating a Monthly Calendar.

NELLIE TALE

In our kitchen we had a large 2' by 3' poster board calendar. It served as a one-month, day-by-day display of everything the family and each individual kid faced: School tests, homework blocks, chores, athletic practices and games, extracurricular events, playdates, parent commitments and family outings and trips.

The boys rotated in gathering the monthly information from each family member under the supervision of a parent. At the beginning of each month a kid filled in the days — the youngest could barely write legibly but there were no excuses. The schedule itself didn't always work precisely but we all took a measure of pride in it. Just seeing one month with each day's activities listed had a perceptively calming effect because each of knew what we were responsible for on any given day.

DESIGNATED CHORES

As Deborah Cohen from the Center for Parenting Education says about the value of chores: "Kids feel more connected and valued when they're counted on…being needed by your family is invaluable. Even though it is more difficult at the time to persist in having children do chores, kids benefit from the experience." (16)

Jennifer Wallace writes in *The Wall Street Journal*, "Those children who do have a set of chores have higher self-esteem, are more responsible, and are better able to deal with frustration and delay gratification, all of which contribute to greater success in school." (17)

More piling on:

"Research by Dr. Marty Rossman, Professor Emeritus at the University of Minnesota School of Education found that involving children in household tasks at an early age can have a positive impact later in life. She found that young adults who began chores at ages 3 and 4 were more likely to have good relationships with family and friends, to achieve academic and early career success and to be self-sufficient, as compared with those who didn't have chores or who started them as teens." (18)

"If you want your children to be intelligent, read them fairy tales. If you want them to be more intelligent, read them more fairy tales." Albert Einstein, theoretical physicist.

READ TO THEM

One of my fondest memories of being a parent was reading to my sons in the evening. They had set bedtimes (one of our routines) and virtually every night of the week we gathered in the eldest's room with a book and read aloud. Our selections were popular kid adventures and included, Laura Ingalls Wilder's *Little House on the Prairie*, *The Hardy Boys* (wayyy old school), *Tucket's Travels: Francis Tucket's Adventures in the West, 1847-1849*, *The Boxcar Children*, *Magic Treehouse* and *The Berenstain Bears*. All were series and stretched for nights through the months and years.

SOCIALIZATION

"Socialization" is the word men and women smarter than me use but it's an apt term. It's plain: Be relentless in getting them back into the social scenes in which they thrived prior to March 2020.

Ease into it but begin the push. On that score, Dr. Dominique A. Phillips of the University of Miami Child and Adolescent Mood and Anxiety Treatment Program, says: "Prolonged avoidance can lead to even more anxiety and less confidence in socializing. Begin with regular interactions with friends and expand to more activities with more friends in more settings… If they're assuming the worst about upcoming contact with others, encourage flexibility and help them develop more realistic expectations. In so many cases, the anxious anticipation is much worse than the reality of a dreaded social interaction." (19)

Moreover, renew your friendships with other parents, starting with the parents of your kids' peers.

GET YOUR KID IN THE ARENA

NELLIE TALE

On Father's Day a year ago, I was fortunate to have Michaeleen Doucleff of *National Public Radio* (NPR) write a feature on my book *Four Lessons From My Three Sons* (yep, #Nohumblebragwhatsoever!) (20) She is the author of a *New York Times* bestseller on parenting and a Mom. (21)

Doucleff focused on a mildly controversial section of my book entitled *Read the Crowd* which outlined how I sent my young sons, with no supervision, into unfamiliar situations. This was a takeoff on my all-time parenting heroine, Lenore Skenazy, whom the national media dubbed the "World's Worst Mom" for letting her nine-year-old son ride the New York subway system alone. (22)

Here is the interview highlight:

<u>Doucleff</u>: In the book, you talk about teaching kids to bounce back after adversity by intentionally creating opportunities for children to encounter obstacles — real-life obstacles — that they have to overcome without a parent's help. Sometimes they even fail a few times before solving the problem. Can you explain a little about these experiences and how you go about creating them for your kids?

<u>Nelligan</u>: Starting when my boys were about 6 or 7, I would play the "change-the-five" game. We'd be in the mall and I'd take three five-dollar bills out of my wallet and hand one to each son. Then I'd say, `Here's the deal, guys. Each of you is going to go into a store and get five dollars change for this. There's no time limit on it. But you've got to walk away from me and do the whole thing alone. And don't come back until you have the change.' I would keep an eye on them and sometimes they would strike out in the first store. Then they would go to others and try again.

I would also have them run into the 7-Eleven and pick up items for me. Again, I'd say something like, `Dad wants these five things, go in and get them.' The first time, of course, they don't want to do it and are like, "Well, Dad ... " And I'd respond, `My man, there's no 'well' about it. Here's the money, memorize what I told you and go get it. I know you can do it.' So, here's this six-year-old kid and he's dealing with a cashier and with other people in line in a strange place. He's doing things that adults do.

And by playing these types of games over and over again, the sons became confident in unfamiliar scenes. And that confidence bleeds over into every aspect of their life…"

In other parts of the interview not aired, I related to Doucleff the following:

All three sons soon became accustomed to this independence. They'd become totally engaged in these "tests" and afterwards they'd be thrilled, as only young boys can be, to talk about their treks. By making it a game, I immediately won the boys' participation.

Fast forward: The eldest at age 15 is at big train station in New Jersey, confused about schedules and noise and surging people. He gets himself calmed down and starts looking around him and sees a kid carrying an orange duffle bag emblazoned with "McDonogh School Athletics." My son has played against this school and thus feels comfortable in introducing himself to the kid and asking advice. It turns out the guy knows all about schedules and points my son to the right train.

"Over-protectiveness is a danger in and of itself. A child who thinks he can't do anything on his own eventually can't."
Lenore Skenazy

Once the youngest son, all of five-years-old, is at a kids' party at a big shopping mall with a pair of hopelessly disorganized parents who drift away with a group of youngsters, leaving my boy and two other kids in the midst of a huge food court. You're a parent – can you imagine the initial panic the kids felt when they realized they were alone?!

But aha, Nellie Junior knows what to do. He recalls what I told him and his brothers once when we were in the surging crowds at a local college football stadium. "You guys are small so if you get lost somewhere in a bunch of people, look for that guy with a stripe running down their pants. That's a policeman or a soldier and they'll you help out." At the mall, my kid tells that to the two other kids and they stare intently at passing legs and after a few minutes, they spot a mall security officer who eventually links them up with the irresponsible parents.

By placing the boys in the areas – the swirling real world – they learned to function and develop self-assurance. I urge you to undertake one of the examples above. And for goodness sake, don't be somewhere and tell yourself you'll do it next time. There's never a next time.

MODEL CONFIDENCE YOURSELF

Here's something that is self-evident: It's always show time when you're a parent. (Recall my humiliating shakedown with my sons over my phone use).

To that end, here are some good, down-to-earth tips on modeling confidence, drawn from the experts at ChildMind.org:

- "Be the example: Seeing you tackle new tasks with optimism and lots of preparation sets a good example for kids.

- You don't have to pretend to be perfect.

- Do acknowledge your anxiety, but don't focus on it—focus on the positive things you are doing to get ready.

- When you put effort into everyday tasks (like raking the leaves, making a meal, cleaning up the dishes, or washing the car), you're setting a good example.

- Give them examples of how you've pushed through the social situation in the past.

- Modeling the right attitude counts too. When you do tasks cheerfully (or at least without grumbling or complaining), you teach your child to do the same. When you avoid rushing through chores and take pride in a job well done, you teach your child to do that too." (23)

TEACH THEM GRATITUDE

There is no more ideal word, counterintuitively, than gratitude in a book examining the compounded and inexcusable wounds inflicted upon youths during the last two years.

Why? Because your kids — and you and me and my kids — were all provided with a stark contrast on how good we had it prior to pandemic lockdowns. I mean here the good in its most basic sense — the freedom to walk outside our front door every morning and proceed unhindered with our daily lives.

Here it is said better than anyone can say it: Amy Morin, editor-In-chief of verywellmind.com: "In a time when many middle school kids carry around $600 phones that they take for granted, teaching gratitude can feel like an uphill battle. But despite the challenges you might face in helping kids feel grateful in a world that seems to value overabundance, it can be worthwhile."

Everyone from Oprah Winfrey to G.K. Chesterton to Willie Nelson to Marcus Aurelius' has a moving exhortation about gratitude, and you know what, each one is true and better yet, uplifting. (24)

And following along with the advice drumbeat of this book, gratitude can be developed.

Below are some tips for teaching Gratitude from First Things First, a superb parenting site.

Nellie Check: I'm one of the most unsentimental men you'll ever meet and I think the below are priceless.

---

1. "Teach them to say thank you to the people who do things for them. That can be their server at a restaurant, a brother or sister who helps them pick up toys, or a friend who gives them a birthday gift.

2. Tell your kids why you are grateful for them. Be specific in letting your children know they are special and loved. For example: 'I appreciate the way you help your brother tie his shoes.'

3. Talk about the things you are grateful for. This can be done in many ways, from a blessing before dinner to keeping a family gratitude journal.

4. Support a charitable event or organization. Whether you are donating clothes or toys, participating in a food drive, or baking cookies for a new neighbor, talk to children about what those actions mean to those who receive the kindness.

5. Be consistent. Like all skills, gratitude is not learned in one lesson."

LEDGER LINE

Reality check: Think again back to the kid you had on January 1, 2020. Then consider your kid today.

I can nearly guarantee nearly two years of lockdowns took a toll on your kid in the confidence and well-being realm. Perhaps, to loop in the prior chapter, it didn't help that virtually all contact with the outside world came through the Interweb. All the data above details the isolation and it's results. Reading it, perhaps you sense that your child has become more insular, more alone and lonely. Perhaps they lost a step or two or three in the ways in which they approach the world outside your front door.

He or she won't change this singlehandedly. Your engagement is key. The instructions are here and they are simple - routines, chores, time spent with them reading, getting them out in the world. And no, on the latter you don't have to start with the Skenazy-Nellie gambit. Just work up to it.

Above all, breakout with patterns that can provide you a new, happy, striving, well-adjusted kid.

Now, we move on to the final cost of lockdown madness.

Footnotes

1. Humor is the best way to spark a kid's interest and it easily beats a tedious recitation of platitudes. Humor also has staying power; ten years later my boys and I laugh about certain experiences they had at age seven and from which they recall well the lessons they learned.

2. Appendix E contains material on the unheeded. For example, The Great Barrington Declaration: "As infectious disease epidemiologists and public health scientists we have grave concerns about the damaging physical and mental health impacts of the prevailing COVID-19 policies, and recommend an approach we call Focused Protection. Coming from both the left and right, and around the world, we have devoted our careers to protecting people. Current lockdown policies are producing devastating effects on short and long-term public health." https://gbdeclaration. org/

3. "When will school open? Here's a state-by-state list," The Today Show, Aug. 20, 2020. https://www.today.com/parents/when-will-school-open-here-s-state-state-list-t179718

4. "Loneliness and mental health in children and adolescents with pre-existing mental health problems: A rapid systematic review," by Emily Hards, Maria Elizabeth Loades, Nina Higson-Sweeney, and Roz Shafran, National Library of Medicine, June 6, 2022 https://pubmed.ncbi.nlm.nih.gov/34529837/#:~:text=Conclusions%3A%20Loneliness%20is%20associated%20with,this%20relationship%20may%20be%20bidirectional. Also, "Rapid Systematic Review: The Impact of Social Isolation and Loneliness on the Mental Health of Children and Adolescents in the Context of COVID-19" by Maria Elizabeth Loades, Eleanor Chatburn, Nina Higson-Sweeney, Shirley Reynolds, and Roz Shafran, National Library of Medicine, November 20, 2020 https://www.ncbi.nlm.nih.gov/pmc/articles/PMC7267797/

5. "Pediatricians, Child and Adolescent Psychiatrists and Children's Hospitals Declare National Emergency in Children's Mental Health," Press Release, October 19, 2021, American Academy of Pediatrics (AAP), the American Academy of Child and Adolescent Psychiatry (AACAP) and the Children's Hospital Association (CHA). https://www.aacap.org/aacap/zLatest_News/Pediatricians_CAPs_Childrens_Hospitals_Declare_National_Emergency_Childrens_Mental_Health.aspx

6. "Children's mental health issues have increased, insurance claims suggest," By Chia-Yi Hou,

The Hill, September 12, 2022. https://thehill.com/changing-america/well-being/mental-health/3634774-childrens-mental-health-issues-have-increased-insurance-claims-suggest/

7. "COVID-19 has made children more worried, scared, and lonely," by Connor Ibettson, January 21, 2020, YouGov UK poll - https://yougov.co.uk/topics/health/articles-reports/2021/01/12/covid-19-has-made-children-more-worried-scared-and

8. "It's a crisis: More children suffering mental health issues, challenges of the pandemic," by Joan Murray, *CBS News*, Aug. 1, 2022. https://www.cbsnews.com/miami/news/crisis-more-children-suffering-mental-health-issues-challenges-pandemic/

9. "'A cry for help': CDC warns of a steep decline in teen mental health / More than 4 in 10 told the health agency they felt 'persistently sad or hopeless'", by Moriah Balingit, *The Washington Post*, March 13, 2022 https://www.washingtonpost.com/education/2022/03/31/student-mental-health-decline-cdc/

10. "CDC study: Abuse, violence, other events linked to poor mental health in teens during COVID pan-demic," by Adrianna Rodriguez, USAToday, October 13, 2022. https://www.usatoday.com/story/news/health/2022/10/13/

cdc-teens-report-poor-mental-health-during-co-vid/10475159002/ The full CDC report is here: https://www.cdc.gov/mmwr/vol-umes/71/wr/mm7141a2.htm?s_cid=mm7141a2_w

11. "Randi Weingarten Flunks the Pandemic / National test results reveal the damage from school clo-sures,' Editorial Board, *The Wall Street Journal*, September 1, 2022. https://www.wsj.com/articles/randi-weingarten-flunks-the-pandemic-naep-test-scores-decline-schools-covid-american-federation-of-teachers-11662069418;

12. "Kids Are Far, Far Behind in School / Educators need a plan ambitious enough to remedy enormous learn-ing losses," By Thomas Kane, Director of the Center for Education Policy Research at Harvard University, *The Atlantic,* May 22, 2022. https://www.theatlantic.com/ideas/archive/2022/05/schools-learning-loss-remote-covid-education/629938/

13. "CDC study: Abuse, violence, other events linked to poor mental health in teens during COVID pan-demic," by Adrianna Rodriguez, *USAToday*, October 13, 2022. https://www.usatoday.com/story/news/health/2022/10/13/cdc-teens-report-poor-mental-health-during-covid/10475159002/ The full CDC report is here: https://www.cdc.gov/mmwr/vol-umes/71/wr/mm7141a2.htm?s_cid=mm7141a2_w

14. "Boundaries, Routines and Early Bedtimes: 13 Habits That Raise Well-Adjusted Kids," by Lauren Tamm, TheMilitaryWifeAndMom.com, April 2022 https://themilitarywifeandmom.com/raise-well-adjusted-kid/

15. "Your Child's Self-Esteem," by D'Arcy Lyness, PhD, Nemours KidsHealth.com, November 2021 https://kidshealth.org/en/parents/self-esteem.html

16. "Family routines: how and why they work," Editors, RaisingChildren.net.au, June 2021 https://raisingchildren.net.au/grown-ups/family-life/routines-rituals-relationships/family-routines#:~:text=Routines%20help%20children%20feel%20safe,well%20planned%2C%20regular%20and%20predictable

17. "The Benefits of Chores," Editors, The Center for Parenting Education, August 2022. https://centerforparentingeducation.org/library-of-articles/responsibility-and-chores/part-i-benefits-of-chores/

18. "Why Children Need Chores / Doing household chores has many benefits—academically, emotionally and even professionally," By Jennifer Wallace, *The Wall Street Journal*, March 13, 2015. https://www.wsj.com/articles/why-children-need-chores-1426262655

19. Ibid.

20. "Here's how to help your kids break out of their pandemic bubble and transition back to being with others" Editors, *The Conversation*, April 15, 2021 https://theconversation.com/heres-how-to-help-your-kids-break-out-of-their-pandemic-bubble-and-transition-back-to-being-with-others-157732

21. "Dad Draws On Māori Roots To Raise 3 Resilient Sons. Step 1: Send Them On A Milk Run" by Michaeleen Doucleff, NPR, June 19, 2021. https://www.npr.org/sections/goatsandsoda/2021/06/19/1007836356/dad-draws-on-maori-roots-to-raise-3-resilient-sons-step-1-send-them-on-a-milk-ru

22. *Hunt, Gather, Parent: What Ancient Cultures Can Teach Us About the Lost Art of Raising Happy, Helpful Little Humans, By Michaeleen Doucleff, March 2021,* https://www.amazon.com/Hunt-Gather-Parent-Ancient-Cultures/dp/1982149671

23. "Parenting Advice From 'America's Worst Mom'by Jane Brody, *The New York Times*, January 15, 2015. My girl Skenazy gives both barrels. https://archive.nytimes.com/well.blogs.nytimes.com/2015/01/19/advice-from-americas-worst-mom/

24. "12 Tips for Raising Confident Kids / How to build self-worth in children and help them feel they

can handle what comes their way" Editors, Child Mind Institute, June 2020 https://childmind.org/article/12-tips-raising-confident-kids/

25. "When I started counting my blessings, my whole life turned around." Willie Nelson / "Be thankful for what you have; you'll end up having more. If you concentrate on what you don't have, you will never, ever have enough." Oprah Winfrey / "Take full account of what Excellencies you possess, and in gratitude remember how you would hanker after them, if you had them not." Marcus Aurelius / "When it comes to life the critical thing is whether you take things for granted or take them with gratitude." G.K. Chesterton

CHAPTER 3

HOW YOU CAN RE-ESTABLISH YOUR KID'S PHYSICAL HEALTH AND FITNESS

"Children are likely to live up to what you believe of them."
Lady Bird Johnson, Former First Lady of the United States

<u>Reality Check</u>: This is going to be a difficult chapter for some parents. Trust me when I say that it is undertaken with compassion and the hope that the material here provides you and your kid with a healthier life forward.

Very few parents want to confront head-on a particular shortcoming of their child. I know I didn't and with three children I had to do it plenty of times.

It goes something like this: At some point in early childhood all the way through preteen to adolescence, you begin to sense and then directly perceive some flaw in your kid's lifestyle or behavior. You will decide to change it and immediately there will ensue pushback, tension, arguments and perhaps the exchange of harsh words. As a close family friend of mine once said, who observed my year-long battle with a son over a lazy approach to school: "Classic case of immovable object meets overwhelming force." She wasn't wrong.

Sure, kids provide you with satisfaction of the deepest kind. But no parents escapes the moments of frustration - which can last days and weeks and months and years - in trying to correct a child's ways.

You probably know where I'm going with this chapter. I told you I was unfiltered and you might be wondering now whether you have the perseverance to hang in there with what we're about to discuss. My advice: Hang in there.

This section begins with a personal anecdote that unbeknownst to me at the time illuminated a disturbing trend that has now hit a crescendo after 20 years. It is difficult and tricky to relate but necessary to illustrate where we find ourselves today.

I was a longtime volunteer assistant coach on my all three of my sons' recreational teams; only and ever an assistant because yes, I knew my own shortcomings. The head coaches were men and women who knew the sports much better than me and were simply better leaders of young kids.

When I began my first tour of duty for my eldest son's soccer team I noticed that there were a few kids on his squad and on others (and this goes for all the teams I helped coach – soccer, basketball, and lacrosse) who were carrying too much weight. It was obvious. There were fleshy rolls around their midsections showing through their jerseys; "soft kids" as my sons would offhandedly and without rancor describe it. (Yes, I already know this is sounding harsh but hear me out.)

I was surprised because the kids in these leagues were pretty young, between the ages of four and six, not preteens or adolescents. Moreover, these were all middle-class kids from our community and I assumed that they, like mine, got a lot of outdoor time and exercise and that their parents provided balanced and nutritious meals. This was in 2001.

Ten years later I was an assistant basketball coach for my youngest son's team and there were more of these "soft kids." Again, not only on my kid's team but on all the teams we faced. And no, I'm no rabid fitness nut or food scold or gym rat with eyes peeled for imperfection; I'm perfectly happy with my Dad's bod, thank you. No, it was simply the observation of a father involved in a lot of community stuff with his kids and their peers.

Enough of this. Nonetheless, it provides a good transition to what was happening prior to and during the pandemic lockdowns.

STATS AND FACTS

My anecdotal observations as an assistant coach were a glimpse of something real.

The Centers for Disease Control and Prevention (CDC) report that before the pandemic lockdowns (2017 to 2020) for children and adolescents aged 2-19 years "...the prevalence of obesity was 19.7% and affected about 14.7 million children and adolescents. Obesity prevalence was 12.7% among 2- to 5-year-olds, 20.7% among 6- to 11-year-olds, and 22.2% among 12- to 19-year-olds." In 2019 the Kaiser Family Foundation chimed in: "Childhood obesity in the United States is a serious public health issue that puts children and adolescents at risk for poor health." (1)

A companion CDC study noted that the rate of young people ages 10 to 19 with type 2 diabetes increased by 95% over the 16-year period, from 2001 to 2017. (2)

Unfortunately, the pandemic lockdowns made these problems worse.

A 2022 article in the Journal of the America Medical Association (JAMA) Network publication noted that youths gained more weight during the COVID-19 pandemic than before it. The greatest change occurred among children aged 5 through 11 years old and the prevalence of overweight or obesity, based on post-pandemic numbers, increased from 36.2% to 45.7%. (3)

Consider that stat: More than four in ten children today are overweight or obese.

And there's more:

Another CDC study of 432,302 children ages 2 to 19 years found the rate of body mass index (BMI) increase nearly doubled during the COVID-19 pandemic compared to the pre-pandemic period. This faster increase was most pronounced in children who were overweight or obese and younger school-aged children overall. (4)

What happens with increased weight gain? Guess.

A decrease in basic fitness. Only 50% of boys and less than 34% of girls ages 12 to 15 today are adequately fit reports CDC. And unfit kids are at risk for cardiovascular and chronic diseases as well as psychological disorders. Moreover, 80% of overweight children become obese adults and "being obese puts a person at risk for many cancers, including colon, breast and endometrial cancers," says Carol Harrison, a senior exercise physiologist at MD Anderson. (5)

In September of 2022, Northwestern University's Dr. Jami Josefson wrote: "As a pediatric endocrinologist at Lurie Children's Hospital, I've seen firsthand an explosion of child obesity among our patients during the pandemic. My colleagues and I have also observed an alarming increase in children with new onset Type 2 diabetes, which is directly related to the widespread weight gain among our patients. In a recent study published in the Journal of Diabetes, my colleagues found that diagnoses of Type 2 diabetes at Lurie increased nearly 300% from the pre-pandemic annual mean." (6)

Who can be surprised?! Lockdowns severed kids from virtually all physical activity found in schools and recess and after-school play and outside sports and playgrounds and daily movement in the world at large. And confined at home, kids had unlimited access to food. (7)

What I had casually glimpsed as assistant rec-league coach was an alarming trend that accelerated fast during the pandemic lockdowns.

Now, consider all of the studies above (and further research is in Appendix D) and here's the sad truth: Too many kids were not in great shape prior to the pandemic and now two years later this problem is worse.

REBOUND
We start with the basics:

"The Physical Activity Guidelines for Americans issued by the U.S. Department of Health and Human Services [where I work, incidentally] recommend that children and adolescents ages 6 through 17 years spend 60 minutes or more doing moderate-to-vigorous physical activity daily. Most of that physical activity should be aerobic, where kids are moving for long periods of time: Participating in daily school athletic periods or on school teams, running around a playground, walking, hiking, and biking [and "dancing around in the living room" as one astute Mom puts it]. "Compared to those who are inactive, physically active youth have higher levels of fitness, lower body fat, and stronger bones and muscles."

"Physical activity also has brain health benefits for school-aged children, including improved cognition (e.g., academic performance, memory) and reduced symptoms of depression. Regular physical activity in childhood and adolescence can also be important for promoting lifelong health and well-being and preventing risk factors for various health conditions like heart disease, obesity, and type 2 diabetes." (8)

C'mon folks, this is basic stuff. Getting your kid moving is essential for his or her quality of life and health and all of the above is as simple as it gets.

And you know what time it is…

THE FAMILY MEETING AND THE PLAN

There's going to be no surprise here: This family meeting will be difficult and touchy. Dr. Julie Snethen, one of the nation's leading experts on childhood obesity, is blunt: "Talking about weight loss is demoralizing to both children and their parents." And she has eminently sensible advice: "The key should be to focus on what we can all do to get healthy. Approach it as a family." (9) She's right. Once you're all in it's easier to change it all.

I'll refrain (mercifully) from the Family Meeting and Plan lecture. You know what to do. Now move.

As with most seemingly impossible things in life, progress begins with basic routines which pursued diligently become lifestyles.

Echo Check: Pursued diligently, basic routines become lifestyles.

LET'S MOVE

I confess I'm a homer for First Lady Michele Obama, who initiated one of the most important national campaigns ever launched, _Let's Move_. (10)

She and her team of White House nutrition and physical activity experts developed and promoted a wide range of healthy activities; these were embraced and expanded by other national advocates, among them Dr. Snethen. Gathered below are tips from _Let's Move_ and others...

- Make a habit of family walks after dinner, walking the dog together (no phones or electronic devices allowed!);

- Set a schedule of chores such as washing the car, mowing the lawn and other yardwork, vacuuming and other housework, doing the breakfast and dinner dishes, cleaning out the basement and garage;

- Give your kids the choice of sustained family activity: Weekend bike rides, family gym memberships, rock-climbing walls (a huge favorite of mine) and martial art classes; erect a stand-alone basketball hoop in the driveway, join swimming and running clubs (there are such clubs for youths); hiking, bowling, yoga classes, ice skating, regular trips to local parks and playgrounds. Bonus: get your kids' friends and other families involved in group outings;

- Inaugurate a 20-minute family morning exercise routine which includes jumping jacks, pushups, sit-ups, running in place. This really good and family-centered idea comes from kidstherapysource.com – it is so worth doing! (11)

"Movement through active free play, especially outside, improves everything from creativity to academic success to emotional stability. Kids who don't get to do this can have so many issues, from problems with emotional regulation—for example, they cry at the drop of a hat—to trouble holding a pencil, to touching other kids using too much force."
Meryl Davids Landau, author of *Enlightened Parenting, A Mom Reflects on Living Spiritually With Kids*, 2016.

- Ensure you have all types of athletic gear in your home and garage – balls of all kinds, hula-hoops (yes), jump ropes, baseball gloves and bats, lacrosse sticks, Frisbees, cones and footwork ladders, badminton and volleyball equipment, rollerblades, skateboards and bikes;

- And there's nothing like good ole family competitions. Have push-up contests, running contests, 10 catches of a football/baseball-without-a-drop challenges, foot races. My sons and I were ferociously competitive - goal-line to goal-line races, 20-yard sprints, who could sink the most consecutive foul shots; how many jumping jacks in a minute. Sometimes it got nutty: who could throw the most wadded-up balls of paper in kitchen garbage can at 10 feet in 30 seconds. And don't get me started about the family bowling sagas.

Every single activity can become one habit and then more habits building toward a consistent pursuit of fun, sustained physical activity.

ORGANIZED SPORTS

These provide a two-fold reward. Not only are the kids kept moving at practice and in games but they also acquire the invaluable intangibles: Camaraderie, working toward a goal and confronting adversity. In every athletic endeavor, individual as well as team sports, *repetition builds character.*

And I don't mean organized sports for just one season a year. I mean two seasons, even three in a year. The grinding discipline learned from a routine of teams and seasons will make them more disciplined in everything else they do.

Moreover, the value of a team and a goal is not found just in formulaic athletic settings. The exact same benefits are present in theatrical productions, music ensembles, marching bands and clubs of all kinds. Kids are energized and excel when they are around other kids with the same interests and motivations.

BEYOND THE FIELDS OF PLAY

And yes, I get it – some kids are not going to be interested in traditional sports. Or some get cut from a team for which they wanted to play (this certainly happened to my kids and it hurt. It hurt them also). In addition, you can't only rely on schools, public or private, to provide all the non-team physical activity a child needs. That's where you have to step up.

If your kid isn't built for team sports it's time to promote individual sports like tennis, gymnastics, marital arts, bicycling, golf, dancing, canoeing, archery, and fishing. Be on the lookout for activities your kid might like. "Keep trying different ideas until something clicks" says Dr. Mary Gavin of Nemours Health. "It's important to get non-athletic kids motivated and moving so they can enjoy a lifelong habit of physical activity."

SET AN EXAMPLE

Michele Obama's campaign was superb precisely because it was aimed both at kids *and parents*. That's why you need to set an example.

You'll learn quickly if you don't know already that breaking a sweat is satisfying and it's even better when your kid is alongside you.

For example, I made it a point every day to get my sons outside in our yard *doing something*. We'd throw the football around or shoot hoops or throw a lacrosse ball back and forth mindlessly or just walk around the neighborhood, shooting the breeze about our days. Sometimes I'd still be in my work-issued suit and tie.

And as a fellow parent, allow me to be blunt: Do not give me this 'But I'm so busy!' jive. I had a full-time job and yet I made the time nearly every early evening to do something – anything - with my sons that involved activity. I know a lot of Dads who did the same thing. This ritual waned when they were on school teams and totally beat after practices. But we always found time on weekends.

One-Note Johnny Check: **Limit time on screens.** Matt Gallagher, a nationally known child fitness guru says: "*The average tween kid spends around seven hours a day texting, posting, tweeting and Instagramming. Think that doesn't matter? A typical kid burns 25 calories an hour sitting and over 160 calories an hour doing light activity. That's a difference of over 800 calories per day!*

Have them shut off their electronics and kids naturally do things that will cause them to be more active." (Emphasis ALL MINE.)

Now, get set because you knew this was coming....

The vital role of diet
Gut check: You can't out-run or out-lift or out-bike or out-swim or out-yoga your daily diet. All the activity and exercise you can muster won't completely defeat what you consume.

Yes, I know the world is awash and crammed and filled with advice on What You Should Eat. In fact, I work for a Federal government agency that practically shrieks at people to eat healthy. Guess what: No one listens. Not even the people who work at my agency.

Here's a super-complicated description of what you should already know:

Proper nutrition is vital for children, not just vital for fat loss and improving fitness but also for healthy growth and decreasing the occurrence of illnesses.

Dietary guidelines
Here's the pronouncement from the mountaintop...

"An underlying premise of the U.S. Department of Agriculture's Dietary Guidelines is that nutritional needs should be met primarily from nutrient-dense foods and beverages. Nutrient-dense foods provide vitamins, minerals, and other health-promoting components and have no or little added sugars, saturated fat, and sodium. A healthy dietary pattern consists of nutrient-dense forms of foods and beverages across all food groups, in recommended amounts, and within calorie limits." I trust you didn't miss the part about 'nutrient-dense.' (12)

Yeah yeah yeah - these are the same dietary guidelines to which few have paid attention for the past three decades. Even a crazy assistant coach knows that.

As with the previous chapters, let's get real with details. Exit generalizations and enter facts. The information below is the most basic you will find in this book – specific and clear and it's what you should provide your kids. Have your kitchen packed with the following...

HERE ARE THE BEST VEGETABLES FOR KIDS
"Bell Peppers, Carrots, Peas, Broccoli, Cauliflower, Spinach, Cucumbers, Celery, Sweet Potatoes, Cherry Tomatoes, Corn, Butternut Squash, Summer Squash, Lettuce, Mushrooms, Asparagus, Avocados, Green Beans, Potatoes."

Why are these the best? "High fiber contents, low-calorie contents, aids to digestion, builds healthy hearts, combats mental illness, improves vision, boosts brain power, improves immune system, full of antioxidants, loaded with vitamins & minerals, improves organ function, help lower blood pressure, *sets up kids for a healthy future diet.*" (13)

An insightful explanation of childhood nutrition comes from the aforementioned Mr. Gallagher, Fitness Director at MFC Sports Performance in Darien, CT:

"A child in my program at the beginning has diet of 80% carbohydrate and half of these carbs are coming from refined white sugar, 5% protein, and 15% fat. I do not have kids count calories or grams...this leads to dietary anxiety and eating disorders for these young, developing minds. I simply ask them to eat certain foods and cut out other certain foods. Foods that children absolutely need to cut out of the diet are foods that are high in sugar or high fructose corn syrup. I have found that once I can get a child to avoid almost all sugar, they instantly lean out and have more energy."

Simple enough?

HERE ARE THE BEST FRUITS FOR KIDS
"Apples, berries — which includes strawberries, blueberries, cherries, and blackberries), bananas, peaches, grapes, pears, pineapples, avocados." (14)

Why are these the best? See above.

Nationally known child nutritionists Dr. Judy Snethen and Deborah Greenberg have two simple suggestions for parents with young children:

"Take the kids shopping with you and see how many different colors you can put into the basket...(and) children are more open to tasting new foods if they help prepare the foods. So involving them in the meal preparation is a good way to help them be more willing to try new foods. Children are also very open to trying new foods that they've grown themselves."

You have the lists of vegetables and fruits above. Now, what about all other foods? Dr. Vincent Iannelli, M.D., a pediatrician and Fellow of the American Academy of Pediatrics, puts it simply: "You begin with forgetting about kid-friendly foods - hot dogs, pizza, French fries, chicken nuggets, juice, and soda."

Below are his recommendations; again, details not generalizations.

"Focus on foods that are high in fiber, low in fat, and have calcium, iron, and other vitamins and minerals."

- *"Breakfast Cereal* - No, not the sugary kind that you simply eat out of the box like candy. Look for whole-grain cereal that is calcium-fortified and has added fiber. Here are five: Cheerios, Multi-Grain Cheerios, Shredded Wheat, Total Raisin Bran, Wheaties." Always add fruit on top;

- *Eggs.* A good source of protein and iron and many other vitamins and minerals;

- *Milk* - a good source of calcium, vitamin D, and protein for kids...should be a part of every child's diet unless they have a milk allergy;

- *Oatmeal* - and oatmeal cookies, oatmeal bars. Oatmeal is a high-fiber food that is good for your kids just like other whole-grain foods;

- *Peanut Butter* - Yes, peanut butter is relatively high in fat, but it is mostly mono- and poly-unsaturated fat, so it is better than the saturated fats that are found in many other high-fat foods. Reduced-fat peanut butter is also available;

- *Yogurt* - is a good source of calcium but not the kids' brands with high sugar. When choosing a yogurt for your kids, look for one with 'live active cultures' that is low-fat and without a lot of added sugar." (15)

<u>Get this in your head:</u> Listed above are 37 — count 'em — healthy foods found in every grocery store on the planet. Here's an easy task for you: The next time you're wheeling your shopping cart down the supermarket aisles, buy just ten of these items above. Bring them home and announce to your kids that this is what the new regime is going to look like. Repeat the sequence, over and over and over. Ask yourself: How hard is this?!

LEDGER LINE

Movement and diet. Two simple two-syllable words. Two vital undertakings. You have the details and facts galore above on how to reverse the physical slide your kid took (and perhaps you as well) during the pandemic lockdowns.

As I said at the top this was not an easy chapter to read nor a funfest to write. That's why I end with this high call for the long game in getting your kid physical healthy and fit.

The most boundless altruism in the world is a parents' devotion to their kids. And that devotion means confronting and then changing some hard realities. Look at your kid right now and get in a time machine. Imagine her or him in five years if their physical and dietary habits continue unabated. Maybe that scares the heck out of you. That should be the wake-up call you need to realize that you've got to work to change these habits. Beginning now.

Footnotes

1. "Children, Obesity, and COVID-19," Centers for Disease Control and Prevention (CDC), June 2022. https://www.cdc.gov/obesity/data/childhood.html

2. "Rates of New Diagnosed Cases of Type 1 and Type 2 Diabetes Continue to Rise Among Children, Teens." CDC, Updated February 2022. https://www.cdc.gov/diabetes/research/reports/children-diabetes-rates-rise.html

3. Changes in Body Mass Index Among Children and Adolescents During the COVID-19, JAMA Research Letter, August 2021. https://jamanetwork.com/journals/jama/fullarticle/2783690

4. "Children, Obesity, and COVID-19" CDC, January 2022. https://www.cdc.gov/obesity/data/children-obesity-COVID-19.html#:~:text=A%20study%20of%20432%2C302%20children,and%20younger%20school%2Daged%20children

5. "10 tips to get kids to exercise / By encouraging your children to exercise every day, you can help them maintain a healthy weight and help prevent diseases like cancer later in life," MD Anderson Health Center, August 2014. https://www.mdanderson.org/

publications/focused-on-health/tips-to-get-kids-to-exercise.h17-1589046.html

6. "Pandemic Surge: Obesity and Diabetes," by Dr. Jami Josefson, Northwestern University, *Chicago Tribune*, September 7, 2022. https://www.chicagotribune.com/opinion/commentary/ct-opinion-pandemic-diabetes-obesity-children-20220927-rklkzlhwo5gil-fmmfm7pso742m-story.html

7. "Screen Time Increases Teenagers' Incidence of Overweight and Obesity," Editors, *Physician's Weekly*, May 2022. https://www.physiciansweekly.com/screen-time-increases-teenagers-incidence-of-over-weight-and-obesity/

8. "Physical Activity Guidelines for School-Aged Children and Adolescents," CDC, July 2022. https://www.cdc.gov/healthyschools/physicalactivity/guidelines.htm#:~:text=The%20Physical%20Activity%20Guidelines%20for,to%2Dvigorous%20physical%20activity%20daily

9. "Pandemic within a pandemic: Childhood obesity rises during COVID shutdown," Dr. Julie Snethen, Director, University of Wisconsin Madison College of Nursing, and Cindy Greenberg, Dean of the College of Health and Human Development at California State University, Fullerton, University of Wisconsin System Notes, April 2022. https://www.

wisconsin.edu/all-in-wisconsin/story/pandemic-within-a-pandemic-childhood-obesity-rises-during-covid-shutdown/

10. The amazing Michele Obama and her "Let's Move! campaign: "America's move to raise a healthier generation of kids." The information here is priceless, timeless, and ideal for parents. https://letsmove.obamawhitehouse.archives.gov/

11. "Kids Exercise List for the Classroom or Home," YourTherapySource.com, August 2022. This is a super breakdown of all the exercise your kid – and YOU – can do at home with little space and no equipment needed. https://www.yourtherapysource.com/blog1/2022/05/26/kids-exercise-list/

12. "Dietary Guidelines for Americans" U.S. Department of Agriculture, August 2022. https://www.nal.usda.gov/legacy/fnic/dietary-guidelines

13. "The 19 Best Vegetables for Kids" Else Nutrition, July 2021. https://elsenutrition.com/blogs/news/19-best-vegetables-for-kids

14. "Top 10 fruits good for kids" Editors, HealthBeginsWithMom.com website. July 2021. https://www.healthbeginswithmom.com/top-10-fruits-good-kids/

15. "The 10 Best Foods for Kids" by Vincent Iannelli, MD, VeryWellFamily.com, June 2020. https://www.verywellfamily.com/best-foods-for-kids-2633967

CHAPTER 4

REINFORCING YOUR KID'S REBOUND: 6 STORIES

"When I was a boy of fourteen, my father was so ignorant I could hardly stand to have the old man around. But when I got to be twenty-one, I was astonished at how much he had learned in seven years." Mark Twain

---

The previous three chapters were hammer blows, proof of the hammering your kid during pandemic lockdowns. They outlined situations and challenges familiar to every parent and some of the content was profoundly disturbing. If what you've read up to now has left you bewildered or angry, take heart, take hope and dig in. You're now completely aware of the territory and you have the maps that will lead you out of it.

We're now going to shift away from the details of Stats and Facts and Footnote Nation to the broader themes of parenting that involve your child's behaviors and attitudes.

Indeed, the past chapters logically flow into this one, from the tight mechanics of how a kid rebounds from the narrow confines of the past to illustrations of how an ever-changing child develops the broader measures of character that orders his or her life ahead.

Hence, what follows is the distillation of observations I've drawn from thousands upon thousands of interactions with parents and kids combined with years of following the work of experts in the fields of parenting, psychology and leadership.

As noted in the Preface, I am a relaxed and loose Dad, a comic in my own mind and the minds of my sons even if with no-one else. I had a years-long habit of using funny exhortations to describe situations and people around which our family found ourselves. You can get away with this with kids – they find a groove in hijinks and goofy repetition. My chief aim in the near non-stop crazy phrases was to highlight compelling moments from which my sons could learn lessons on how to conduct themselves in the relentless real world, which begins when they awake every morning.

The six brief vignettes below highlight a few of my light-hearted and sometimes sophomoric sayings. Some are a bit raw and unusual but all illuminate how character is built and reinforced in children and adolescents. You can take them or leave them inasmuch as some might not fit your specific family style. The hope is that they provide you with ideas on furthering your child's escape from the lockdown bunker-mentality.

And, trust me. Every single situation occurred and as you'll read, no one was spared, not even me. Most of all, the tales are proof that parenting doesn't always have to be a humorless grind forward.

The proof in performance
The power of humor
The strength of calm in adversity
The value of public judging
The beauty of self-awareness
The benefit of explanations in solitude

The proof in performance
"'Diversity, Justice, Inclusiveness.' Yeah, don't forget GPA, SATs, All-Conference."

The first three words above were adorned on banners along the entrance to a high-end prep school in the Mid-Atlantic, symbols of the institution's creed. We were there at 8 a.m. for a Sunday lacrosse tournament.

The last six words were what I added after reading aloud the first three. Sitting in the front seat of the car, my young son instantly grinned and laughed.

The school's slogans are perfectly noble and prime catchwords of a sensitive age. It's nice that young people are encouraged to think about high ideals and act accordingly. But to me the slogans underscored an ethos, however well-meaning, that really didn't cut it in the life of a child. In my hopelessly narrow world, there were other markings – what really counts is doing, not feeling.

Perhaps a kid's life should not be consumed by saluting pop, voguish, beliefs-of-the-day. Maybe a few or a lot of parents – *consumed themselves with ensuring that their child can read, write and do math, have worthy friends and pursue worthwhile activities* – think the same way. And maybe that's why a 10-year-old kid confronted with the stark juxtaposition of the words above laughs out loud.

I chuckled as well and then said, "Hey son, you know your old man likes diversity and justice just fine. But there's a helluva lot more. Like just getting it done."

"That's what we gotta do today against Gilman" he replied.

"Bingo, my man," I responded. "The world – and I mean me, the neighbors, your friends and teachers and coaches – are always looking at you, seeing how you maneuver and perform. That's the way life works. Attitude and skills and hustle and effort are how you are judged. Don't ever forget it."

Yeah, strong stuff for a 10-year-old kid. But he got it. Indeed, he was about to play in a tournament where teams won because they had good, tough players, not because they were righteous or woke. The world rewards and respects accomplishment. Period. If you think otherwise, paste on a big smile when your kid announces he or she has just failed a class.

"A dream doesn't become reality through magic; it takes sweat, determination and hard work." Colin Powell

---

And no, I wasn't dismissive of basic civic virtue. For example, I required all three sons to participate in community service. I compelled them to visit senior assisted centers and listen patiently to the stories of the elderly. I demanded that they go to local schools and help tutor disadvantaged kids in math and English. I stood next to them at food banks handing out lunches to folks down on their luck. Good Lord, you want to talk about the real world? You want to talk about staring human behavior and choices straight in the eye? The boys would come back from these events more thoughtful - and more world-wise - than ever.

Years later, that same son and I were at that same school for one of his last high school football games. His team lost the game and he played badly and we both knew this wasn't going to be a fun ride home. We were driving out of the school at dusk when despite his sour mood, he chuckled and pointed out the car window at one of the aforementioned banners. Spontaneously, I read aloud the first three words. From memory, having heard my pointed, six-word exhortation innumerable times, he laughed and filled in the rest.

The power of humor
"For God's sake, I don't want the *heel*."

Those were the words of an exasperated lady spoken to a scowling supermarket butcher as he sliced up a foot-long salami for her, prompting a hilarious back and forth between the two to which my son listened. I wasn't present at this family classic but it provided a lot of laughs and became the prompt for many such stories in the years after.

Virtually every weekend the four of us accompanied by a host of friends would go to the local high school and play football and lacrosse and chase each other around on the deserted fields for hours, even in the colder months.

Part of this ritual was lunch, very plain fare eaten at the field. On the day of salami woman it was the middle kid's turn to get lunchmeat while the others got French bread and cream soda. My son came back to us at the check-out line and laid out the story with a perfect, high-pitched mimic of the impatient lady and the butcher.

We all loved it – it was a genuinely funny tale and this sometimes-stoic son was genuinely excited as he told it. I was so surprised and pleased with the recitation of the scene that I told the boys I'd give them a dollar every time they had a funny story about something that they'd seen. "See how your brother got that one? Guys, the world is full of these kinds of crazy situations and people and jokes. Keep alert and go out and find them." Obviously, the dollar was symbolic to both them and me - the real thrill was in them bringing back something to share.

Of course, it helped that I acted like a joker sometimes as well. When we'd go to a burger place, or Mexican restaurant or a pizza joint, I'd order a taco at the first, a pizza at the second, and a burger at the last. Then I'd make a confused scene, feigning surprise when I received the obvious answer to my question - "We don't serve that" - from the waiter. The boys knew this rigamarole was going to play out and would be giggling in anticipation. Hey, it wasn't high comedy but it was a funny enough to us.

Once the eldest told us about seeing a woman accidentally back her car into another and when challenged, she told the guy that the massive dent she had just caused in his driver's side-door panel, and the resulting debris on the ground, "had always been there." The kid was excited to tell us and it was a funny story. Pay the man, Shirley.

And I was always ready to surprise them; again, it's easy to be loose in front of your children, any children. During halftime at one of the eldest son's games I was carrying a lacrosse stick I'd found lying near a car in the parking lot. The middle kid and his friends walked by me on the sidelines and my son's face lit up in surprise. "Dad, what are you doing with that stick?" I responded nonchalantly, "I'm gonna warm-up Wheeler," who was the varsity goalie.

Immediately, the kid and his pals could see the whole scene was so patently preposterous – the old man in a suit and tie, shuffling out on a field in front of 200 spectators to take practice shots on a premier goalie - that he and his friends broke out into huge gales laughter. "Gonna warm up Wheeler" became a family staple. Of course I fell short a few times going for the yuk but I was always trying.

The most pleasing and important aspect of this whole exercise is that the boys often looked for something funny when we were out and about. This not only furthered their situational awareness but contributed to their upbeat outlook. "Dad, how about this one – I saw these two guys at school trying to carry a…" Our many times together in the everyday world – and man, get it in your head that's where we all live – could sometimes verge on laugh-a-minute type affairs, three good-natured kids quick with a smile and seeking a gag. You don't simply have kids like this, you develop them. Kids who view the world through the lens of humor are seeing the good and absorbing a lot more.

The strength of calm in adversity
"Yeah, it's the end of the world."

It was a chilly November Sunday at the high school with the Nelligan Four. We'd had contests to see which duo could get 50 consecutive throws of a lacrosse ball without a drop, played the end-zone tackling game, kicked footballs through the uprights using my left shoe as a tee and ran sprints up and down field.

Most fun of all was throwing routes to the boys, even though I have an erratic arm.

The afternoon was winding down and as a regular ritual end to the weekend, I said, "Hey, two more completions and let's go get those donuts. Go long, bud" I said to a kid and then I unleashed a rainbow down field.

As the middle kid maneuvered under the long throw, the two others were visibly upset. "But Dad," said the eldest in desperation, "You got fired from your job!"

"Yeah, it's the end of the world," I replied automatically, watching my pass sail three feet beyond the middle kid's out-stretched arms.

Junior was correct - I had just been fired, a casualty of what happens when your guy finishes on the south side of an election. It was true adversity (what the kid didn't even know was the dim employment picture for my particular skills) and the whole family was increasingly anxious about finances, which was captured by my son's comment.

"OK men, let's have a seat in my office" I told them and we sprawled out at the 50-yard line. "Look guys, I'm not going to give you any fairy tales. Yeah, we all know I'm out of work. But I'll find a job — you know I'm gonna rally. I have you guys to keep me company and besides, you saw me at QB today — I need to work on my deep ball. So yeah, it's the end of the world.

Now let's go get those donuts and when we can't afford them I'll let you know."

"It's the end of the world." What a ridiculous, crazy laconic utterance, framed between a lost job and a bad pass. I couldn't ignore the obvious but I was determined to set an example of calm and lower the temperature. Perspective, folks: Nothing is ever as bad as it seems. Everyone has tough times and there are only three choices: Lie to yourself, wallow in self-pity, or drive forward.

Acknowledging my situation with equanimity was the best way to prove a point to the boys and the light, sardonic utterance had an effect. "Yeah, it's the end of the world." It completely deflated the drama balloon. Almost instantly the boys began repeating it about their small and big problems. I began to see that their using the phrase out loud gave them an immediate face-saving device, deflecting their own worry and embarrassment; it made the child feel better about whatever bind they were in. No hysterics, no spectacles, no day-long despair. Rather, grudging acceptance with levity, however manufactured, and a sign that the kid had controlled the anxiety and that he was ready for the next step.

Seven years later it was summer and we were at the same field on which I'd proved a second-rate QB but a candid Dad. The boys were bigger, faster and stronger and I was employed (thank God the post-election unemployment hadn't lasted too long). We were horsing around, doing sprints from goal line to goal line and whereas years ago I could hold my own, now even the youngest was beating the old man. Afterwards, we were lying on the turf, all four of us exhausted and satisfied, staring at a clear afternoon sky. The eldest son observed, "Dad, we're all faster than you now." "Yeah," I replied, "it's the end of the world," prompting howls of laughter.

The value of public judging
"Don't ever end up like that jackass."

I once saw a kid leave a football field with his Mom holding his helmet and his Dad holding his big equipment bag while the kid, walking ten feet ahead of them, texted furiously on his cell phone. My youngest boy had just played in the same game and the other two sons - all four of us - were ambling back to the parking lot. I stopped them and said "Wait up, guys. Check out that scene," and nodded at zombie screen-boy and the two Sherpa parents. I pointed defiantly at the kid and said, "Don't ever end up like that jackass."

Yep, Dad bringing it in hot! But c'mon, every parent reading this knows of or has seen that jackass kid.

My comment was a take on the phrase "If you see something, say something" and my boys always knew the old man would do so. There are no judgment-free zones in my life or in anyone's life for that matter.

When my boys and I were out and about in the real world I genuinely treasure my head was on a swivel seeking metaphors in everything and everyone, relentless in acknowledging good and bad. When we watched a football game and a receiver scored a touchdown and didn't dance around in the end zone like a fool but instead simply dropped the ball and ran to the sideline, I'd say, "Check that guy out – he's not drawing attention to himself or embarrassing the guy he scored on. There's your class act." I'd point out men and women holding open doors for seniors or a parent gracefully include shy parents in conversation. I'd pull the sons aside and say, "See how Charlie's dad is talking to everyone over there? Remember that." Or, I'd single out the impatient adult in the grocery store being rude to a clerk. "Did you see that jerk? Don't you ever treat anyone that way."

I can hear it now: 'It's not fair to judge others! It's wrong!' Puhhleease. Every single one of us makes judgements every waking hour – that's the way an individual navigates through day-to-day work and life. When you see grace, ensure your kids are aware of it. When you see the opposite, drive home that it's wrong.

To make a real impression on a kid you need to bring it in fast and unfiltered. Examples from the real world work because you don't have to manufacture or fake anything. Daily life relentlessly offers up situations where you encounter and judge the good and the bad and the inspirational in human nature. And why shouldn't you? Like I said, see something, say something. Platitudes uttered to kid in a vacuum are hot air; the real world is as solid as a brick.

The beauty of self-awareness
"Just get the ball to Louie!"

The boys once had a coach named Mark Dubick, a neighbor and a former college lacrosse star. The boys were aware of my total respect for the guy and once when the three of us were driving home from a practice the eldest son asked, "Dad, why do you like Coach Dubick so much?" "Because he's exactly like my old Drill Sergeant Harrison," I responded, "Except Coach is short, white, and Jewish."

Dubick personally selected a top-caliber lacrosse team from about 150 kids at a tryout. Every kid on the final team was good; there was one kid who was great – Louie, Coach Dubick's son.

When things in a game got tight, there was one hoarse, penetrating yell you could count on: "Just get the ball to Louie!" I can still hear it in my mind and see Coach Dubick, always unshaven, gesturing wildly with his clipboard. Far from being some crazed Dad, he was exactly right. Louie was that rare player who could score at crunch time. He was one reason the team was 37-0-1. When the heat was on, Louie gave us the best chance to win and every kid and parent knew it.

Driving back from games, we'd talk about it all and sometimes mimic Coach Dubick's 'Just get the ball to Louie!' It wasn't in jest because we all respected the guy.

It was a classic phrase and one day I decided to make a point. "You know guys, we always hear Coach yelling for Louie when the team's in a hole. But you know why? Because" and here I pointed at my eldest son, Louie's teammate, "we know what he can do and you can't do. Louie scores. You play defense. You both are good at what you do. The key is, on the field and in any situation you are in, you gotta know how you fit into it all and how you can help the overall effort. You gotta be self-aware and that means when you're on the field you gotta work to get the ball to Louie."

The explanation made sense to them; each one – *and every kid* – is in a huge variety of social situations every hour of the day. Each one challenges a child to know how and where they fit in.

Emphasis Check: This is a landscape wayyy beyond the athletic fields – it's the whole child and adolescent world.

The most obvious settings are the easiest: In a classroom, it means respectful behavior and expending effort. In social situations, knowing your role means getting along, being genuine, contributing to a peer group with conversation and humor but also listening more than speaking. Self-awareness marks that kid who knows himself and hence doesn't yield to the pressure to do something stupid.

One of the most important conversations I ever had with my middle son consisted of eight words. He called me from a friend's house at 10 p.m. one evening, an hour before I was to pick him up. "Hey Dad, you need to come get me right now."

Driving him home, my son explained that some unknown kids had showed up at the house and started drinking. My kid put the whole scene in perspective in an instant and panicked: Totally illegal behavior, parents letting it slide, kids getting drunk. Maybe the police. He knew his role alright – get the hell out of there.

The older they got the more self-aware they became. And a few times that meant big-time reproach for Dad (I told you I'd be brutally honest). When the eldest was in 9th grade, I goaded – there's no other word – him about running for a student government office at school. "Hey guy, you have a lot of friends, you're a pretty good talker, you really oughta run for something." He kept demurring and of course, irritating Dad that I was, I kept at it, not even considering that he was fine with who he was at school and what he was doing.

Then one day, in the midst of another round of my nagging, he looked at me long and hard and said, "Dad, I'm getting the ball to Louie." I was stunned, and silenced. And that was that.

Explanations in Solitude

Beginning when the eldest was in third grade, I took great care in explaining to each kid individually the basic personal qualities to which I wanted them to aspire.

How and Where was key: They were too young for high-sounding lectures on courtesy, self-awareness, reliability and confidence. No kid is going to understand that stratospheric approach. It has to be simple and the tales you've read have that simplicity.

Furthermore, it's imperative you have your child's full, undivided attention. This rules out a room in the house or the backyard porch or a restaurant or a shopping mall or the front seat of a car. Hence, to have these conversations I used an ideal setting of peace and quiet, one with no distractions: Saturday mornings in the bleachers fronting the fields of our local high school, a poignant, solitary venue.

As we sat together, I would engage them first with simple queries to get them loose - who are your favorite teachers? Subjects? If you could have one car, what would it be? What's the best burger you've ever had? If you could choose one book to read what would it be? What is your big win of the week? And of course, "why?" after every question to drag the conversations out further. Then, I'd gently guide the talk to the topics you've just read about (and others). Children are naturally curious and a small amount of prompting will get them going for a long time. I know - because the boys began to look forward to these Saturdays and the long talks about anything and everything. It was a fond ritual and believe it or not, these explanations in solitude persist to this day.

LEDGER LINE

Every single parent has stories about their kids, turning-point tales that signaled major shifts in their child's growth. I know you could easily match the stories above with some of your own.

I trust you didn't find the tales outrageous or unbelievable. Because while some are outrageous, believe me, all of this really happened. Indeed, these six tales encapsulate the entire thrust of my parenting: The constant search for situations in the real world that would make a lasting impression on my sons in their world, helping them become reflexive in making the right decision when nothing was on the line and when everything was on the line.

Most important, I trust the themes here regarding attitude and behavior — that's right, character - assist as you begin to help your kid climb back out of the lockdown quagmire.

Now we'll drive into the final chapter, fittingly, The Last Ledger Line...

CHAPTER 5

THE LAST LEDGER LINE

Do not wait; the time will never be 'just right.' Winston Churchill

---

One of my kids once said to me, commenting on an unfortunate and sustained series of bad decisions made by a close family friend, "I've never seen a train wreck last so long."

It's an ideal metaphor for the pandemic lockdowns, which were the result of a series of perplexing, grotesque and sometimes fantastical decisions whose aftermath we will deal with for years to come. The near complete shuttering of American society paralleled by a cruel environment of fear (erratically still continued in some regions of the country) affected us all but the harshest blows fell upon our children. Not a single kid was left untouched.

This book covered what I - and many others more knowledge-able and sophisticated than me - saw as three significant areas of lockdown damage to youths: Digital media usage, mental well-being and confidence, and physical health and fitness. This conclusion is fully supported by research, evidence, and data and more about these catastrophes is revealed every day. Equally important, these were the areas with which the hundreds and hundreds of parents to whom I spoke were most concerned. There are no doubt other areas of life that were affected; every parent has a story.

As noted at the beginning, the strength of this book is that it consolidates in one slender volume the extent of the damage, but most importantly, it brings to one place the wealth of good and sensible advice from respected and knowledgeable profes-sionals - advice that was heretofore widely dispersed and hence, did not have the impact it deserved or deserves.

There are two takeaways from this book. The first is that it contains a sheer amount of information and common sense - the challenges you face are explained; the instructions for change are straightforward. There's enough to keep you and your fam-ily going for years.

Last Reality Check: Notice the "you" in that previous sentence.

The second and most important takeaway, clearly and cleanly explained throughout, involves you.

It is up to you to get this machinery started and begin...wait for it...Your Kid's Rebound from Pandemic Lockdowns. No kid I have ever known would voluntarily and happily undertake by themselves the steps outlined here. They are kids and to reiterate what was said before, you are the adult. You're in charge.

The train wreck of lockdowns is finally screeching to a halt. As it does, I trust this book brought into sharp focus the changes in your child that you had casually or more closely perceived and that those changes are troubling enough to provide inspiration for your move to action. As I said at the beginning, no-one has all the answers. But here you have enough to get your child to Rebound.

Don't take my word for it. Prove me right.

SAMPLES OF FAMILY CELL PHONE CONTRACTS

B elow are three samples of cell phone contracts between a parent and their child. Why three?

Parents and family have different styles of operation. You'll find that each of these contracts has varying goals, responsibilities and consequences. I trust one or a mix of the three fits your family situation.

The first is from Jennifer O'Donnell and the VeryWellFamily. com website; her bio: "Jennifer O'Donnell is a former writer for Verywell Family covering tween parenting. She has covered parenting and child rearing for more than 8 years as an online writer. She digs camping, family movie nights, and yoga. She has been an active volunteer with a children's service organization since 2001, working primarily with tweens and teens. On parenting she says: 'There's so much to enjoy and a lot to worry about. Find a balance and choose your battles carefully.'"

Sample Cell Phone Contract for Parents and Tweens

By Jennifer O'Donnell / July 30, 2021

Deciding if your tween is responsible enough to have a cell phone isn't always an easy decision to make. And once you've made it, you will still need to teach your child some basic rules of cell phone ownership, as well as the responsibilities that come with having a cell phone.

Creating a cell phone contract between you and your tween is an excellent way to teach your child about these rules and responsibilities, as well as the consequences for not seeing them through. Be sure you go over every item in your contract, giving your child the opportunity to ask questions and even make suggestions.

The sample phone contract below can get you and your child started. Use the contract as is, or edit it according to your own rules and consequences. Review the contract together periodically, as circumstances and challenges may change.

SAMPLE CELL PHONE CONTRACT

This contract between [Parents' Names Go Here] and [Tween's Name Goes Here] establishes family rules and consequences regarding cell phone usage.

[Tween's Name] Cell Phone Responsibilities

Make a list of your child's responsibilities, such as:

- I will share my phone's password with my parents and they may use it to check my phone at any time.

- I will not send threatening or mean texts to others.

- I will not text or place phone calls after 9 p.m.

- I will keep my phone charged at all times.

- I will answer or respond promptly when my parents contact me.

- I will not bring my cell phone to the family dinner table.

- I will not go over our plan's monthly minutes or text message limits. If I do, I understand that I may be responsible for paying any additional charges or that I may lose my cell phone privileges.

- I understand that I am responsible for knowing where my phone is, and for keeping it in good condition.

- I will obey the rules of etiquette regarding cell phones in public places. I will make sure my phone is turned off when I am in church, restaurants, or other quiet settings.

- I will obey any rules my school has regarding cell phones, such as turning them off during class, or keeping them on vibrate while riding the school bus.

- I will alert my parents when I receive suspicious or alarming phone calls or text messages from people I don't know.

- I will also alert my parents if I am being harassed by someone via my cell phone.

- I will not use my cell phone to bully another person.

- I will send no more than _____ texts per day.

- I understand that having a cell phone can be helpful in an emergency, but I know that I must still practice good judgment and make good choices that will keep me out of trouble and out of danger.

- I will not send embarrassing photos of my family or friends to others. In addition, I will not use my phone's camera to take embarrassing photos of others.

- I will not use my phone to buy or download anything without asking permission first.

CONSEQUENCES

Then, include the consequences for breaking cell phone usage rules:

- I understand that having a cell phone is a privilege and that if I fail to adhere to this contract, my cell phone privilege may be revoked.

- If needed, I may help pay for the cost of the phone and/ or for excess charges that I incur without permission from my parents.

- I understand that my cell phone may be taken away if I talk back to my parents, fail to do my chores, or fail to keep my grades up.

PARENT RESPONSIBILITIES

Finally, detail the parent responsibilities, including:

- I understand that I will make myself available to answer any questions my child might have about owning a cell phone and using it responsibly.

- I will support my child when they alert me to an alarming message that they have received.

- I will alert my child if our cell phone plan changes and impacts the plan's minutes.

- I will give my child _____ warning(s) before I take his or her cell phone away.

Signed _____ [Child / Tween / Teen]

Signed _____ [Parents]

Date _____

Source: https://www.verywellfamily.com/a-sample-cell-phone-contract-for-parents-and-tweens-3288540

The second sample contract is from Sean Grover and appeared in *Psychology Today*; his bio: "A psychotherapist and author with over 25 years of experience with kids and parents. He is a designer of award-winning youth programs and leads one of the largest group therapy practices in the United States, in addition to monthly workshops in clinics, medical centers, youth organizations, and schools."

"The Best Technology-Screen Time Contract for Kids" by Sean Glover

Kids crave structure, consistency, and leadership from parents. So rather than go to war over screen time, I recommend establishing a family culture around technology by sitting down and creating a Family Screen Time Contract.

The contract below provides a basic framework, allowing for flexibility and customization based on your kids' ages and your family's use of technology. Set aside a time to fill it in together, edit it, or use it as a jumping off point for discussion. Each family is different, so each contact will be too.

Remember, the contract is not a punishment but a way to set healthy screen time boundaries for everyone in your family, including parents. Screen time devices include smartphones, computers, laptops, televisions and all game systems.

THE _____ FAMILY SCREEN TIME CONTRACT

1. School Nights & Weeknights

Our family shuts down all our devices at _____ o'clock. The devices remain off until the next morning. Devices will not be turned back on until everyone has finished breakfast, and is dressed and ready to leave.

2. Weekends & Holidays

Our family limits screen time on weekends and holidays to _____ hours/minutes per day.

3. Travel Vacations

After arriving at our destination, everyone in our family limits screen time to _____ minutes in the morning and _____ minutes in the evening. We leave our devices in our hotel or vacation homes and don't take them on activities, such as hiking, going to the beach, cycling, etc. If needed, one device may be designated to be used for directions, photos ,or emergency calls.

4. Screen Time Blackouts

Our family does not use our devices when we have: (check all that apply)

____ Meals together

____ Family gatherings

____ Friends visiting

____ Playdates

____ Sleepovers

____ To walk or drive

Add your personal family guidelines here:

_____

5. Device Storage & Charging

Our family does not store or charge tech devices in our bed-rooms or playrooms. Instead, we keep our devices in a communal space, which is... _____.

6. Screen Time Privilege

Devices aren't available after school until homework and chores are completed. Chores may include:

____ Making beds

____ Tidying up rooms

____ Doing dishes

____ Taking care of <u>pets</u>

____ Helping prepare dinner

Add your additional family chores here:

_____

7. Alternatives to Screen Time

Our family recognizes that too much screen time is unhealthy. As a family, we each have weekly physical and creative activities such as (check at least three):

____ Exercise

___ Sports

___ Musical instruments

___ Art

___ Dance

___ Reading for pleasure

Add your own special activities here:

_____

Signed _____

Source: https://www.psychologytoday.com/
us/blog/when-kids-call-the-shots/201804/
the-best-technology-screen-time-contract-kids

_____

The third sample is from the irrepressible Josh Shipp, a well-known parenting commentator. I'll share his bio again: "Statistically, Josh Shipp should be dead, in jail, or homeless. But his success as a preeminent author, speaker, and global youth empowerment expert is living proof of the power of one caring adult. A former at-risk foster kid turned youth advocate, Josh is renowned for the documentary TV series on A&E that followed his groundbreaking work with youth and families."

CELL PHONE AGREEMENT

Dear Caring Adult,

This contract is designed to create an open line of communication between you and your kid regarding their cell phone.

The goal is to help your kid become a well-rounded person who can coexist with technology, NOT be ruled by it.

You probably find yourself in one of two situations:

1. They already have a cell phone with no clear rules in place.

Expect the conversation to be a bit tougher here. They will feel you are setting the ground rules after the game has begun. Admit that you made a mistake (we all do) and that because you care about them(which you do), that's why we are doing this.

2. You're about to give them a cell phone.

GOOD NEWS! There is no better time to get people to agree to what you want, than when you're handing them a shiny new toy. "I just need you to review and sign this understanding about your cell phone -- then it's all yours!"

Edit the contract on the next page as needed to make it your own.

Encourage your kid to ask questions…

and don't be afraid to have a few laughs along the way.

Cheers,
Josh Shipp
Founder, OneCaringAdult

Dear _____,

CONGRATS! You've proven yourself mature and responsible enough for your own cell phone. Given that you have a new cell phone in your hands, we obviously trust you to make good decisions—so why are we making you sign this lame thing that's loaded with stuff that you probably already know?

Well, let me get to the point.

A cell phone is more than a piece of technology. If used wrongly, it can be a weapon that puts your safety at risk. You've always been a great kid, and we want to make sure that you continue making smart choices.

The goal of this agreement is to make sure that you're always safe and happy—and that we always maintain a direct and open line of communication. I'm asking you to always use your phone for good and to ask for help from me or a trusted adult when a situation leaves you feeling scared or unsure.

I. CELL PHONE AGREEMENT - RULES

1) I understand that the rules below are for my safety and that my parents love me more than anything in the world. I understand that my parents want to give me freedom, while also giving me enough security to make smart choices. **Initial here:** _____

2) I promise that my parents will always know my phone passwords. I understand that my parents have a right to look at my phone whenever there's a need for them to do so, even without my permission.

Initial here: _____

3) I will hand the phone to one of my parents promptly at _____ pm every school night and every weekend night at _____ pm. I will get it back at _____ am. **Initial here:** _____

4) I will not send or receive naked photos. Ever. I understand that there could be serious legal consequences that could put mine and my parents' future at-risk. **Initial here:** _____

5) I will never search for porn or anything else that I wouldn't want my grandma finding. **Initial here:** _____

6) I understand that my behavior on my phone can impact my future reputation—even in ways that I am not able to predict or see. **Initial here:** _____

7) I will tell my parents when I receive suspicious or alarming phone calls or text messages from people I don't know. I will also tell my parents if I am being harassed by someone via my cell phone. **Initial here:** _____

8) When I'm old enough, I won't text and drive. I understand it's dangerous and stupid. **Initial here:** _____

9) I will turn off, silence, and put my phone away in public—especially in a restaurant, at the movies, or while speaking with another human being. I am not a rude person. I will not allow the phone to change this important part of who I am. **Initial here:** _____

10) I will NEVER use my phone to bully or tease anyone, even if others think it's funny. **Initial here:** _____

I understand that having this phone is not a right—it is a privilege that can be taken away. As such, I have read the following document and agree to the above rules. I understand that if I have any questions, I should ask.

_____

Sign here

II. CELL PHONE AGREEMENT - CONSEQUENCES

Violation	Consequence
1st time	☐ Loss of the device I broke the rule with for 6-days ☐ Sit-down discussion
2nd time	☐ Loss of the device I broke the rule with for one week ☐ Sit-down discussion
3rd time	☐ Loss of the device I broke the rule with for two weeks ☐ Sit-down discussion
4th time (or if the violation is unlawful)	☐ Loss of the device I broke the rule with until further notice. ☐ In order to regain use of the device, I should be able to make a clear case about what will be different moving forward. ☐ Consider the help of a professional counselor to help get to the underlying cause of disregard for the rules.

I understand that having this phone is not a right—it is a privilege that can be taken away. As such, I have read the following document and agree to the above consequences.

I understand that if I have any questions, I should ask.

Signatures Here _____

Date _____

More Exploration of the Cyberverse

Overview

This Appendix consolidates some tthe keenest writings on the vast digital media landscape. It was assembled with two goals:

1. Providing you with additional information on the themes in Chapter 2; and,

2. Offering you invaluable (yep, my word) resources to reduce the digital media usage of your family.

The Experts

If you want the best – and the last – word on youth and digital media go to Dr. Jean Twenge and Dr. Jonathan Haidt. Below are the highlights of their work.

All things Twenge – www.JeanTwenge.com – her writing, books, and research. Of particular note is a compendium of her research into youth and digital media, found here: http://www.jeantwenge.com/research/

Her *New York Times* Bestseller: *iGen: Why Today's Super-Connected Kids Are Growing Up Less Rebellious, More Tolerant, Less Happy--and Completely Unprepared for Adulthood--and What That Means for the Rest of Us*, 2017 / (available on Amazon).

Dr. Jonathan Haidt - This piece by Dr. Haidt received national attention when it appeared: "The Dangerous Experiment on Teen Girls; The preponderance of the evidence suggests that social media is causing real damage to adolescents," by Jonathan Haidt, *The Atlantic*, Nov. 21, 2021. This is long, detailed and devastating. A must read if you have a daughter.

https://www.theatlantic.com/ideas/archive/2021/11/facebooks-dangerous-experiment-teen-girls/620767/

His *New York Times Bestseller: The Coddling of the American Mind: How Good Intentions and Bad Ideas Are Setting Up a Generation for Failure*, 2018 (available on Amazon) looks at the proclivities of the youngest Millennials and GenX.

Finally, the Duo: "This Is Our Chance to Pull Teenagers Out of the Smartphone Trap," *The New York Times*, July 31, 2021, by Dr. Jean Twenge and Dr. Jonathan Haidt. This piece sums it all up in superb fashion.

https://www.nytimes.com/2021/07/31/opinion/smartphone-iphone-social-media-isolation.html

---

Two other leading commentators with outstanding observations on navigating youth through the digital world:

Dr. Devorah Heitner, CEO of Raising Digital Citizenship; her website is https://devorahheitner.com/ She is the author of *Screenwise: Helping Kids Thrive (and Survive) in Their Digital World*, 2016 (available on Amazon).

Diana Graber is chief of Cyerberwise at https://www.cyber-wise.org/ and is the coauthor of *Raising Humans in a Digital World: Helping Kids Build a Healthy Relationship with Technology*, 2019 (available on Amazon).

SELECT ARTICLES ON CHILDREN AND DIGITAL MEDIA

1. "Social Media Use in Children and Adolescents," *Journal of American Medical Association*, May 31, 2022. A data-driven dive in kids and screens.

https://jamanetwork.com/journals/jamapediatrics/fullarticle/2792736#:~:text=Some%20evidence%20suggests%20that%20some,concerns%20should%20also%20be%20considered.

2. 2022 Cell Phone Usage Statistics: How Obsessed Are We? By Trevor Wheelwright, *Reviews.org*, Jan. 22, 2022. This article is as alarming as it is despairing. https://www.reviews.org/mobile/cell-phone-addiction/#:~:text=How%20often%20are%20we%20using,phones%20are%20our%20constant%20companions

3. CommonSenseMedia.org is a superb resource for parents on all things Internet. For example: "The Common Sense Census: Media Use by Tweens and Teens," March 9, 2022. Get ready to get surprised. https://www.commonsensemedia.org/research/the-common-sense-census-media-use-by-tweens-and-teens-2021

4. "State of Kids' Privacy Report 2021," Common Sense Media, November 16, 2021. More stats…and more alarms. https://www.commonsensemedia.org/research/state-of-kids-privacy-report-2021

5. "Pills for the Girls / Why does every harmful social media trend snag young women?" by Carmel Richardson, *The American Conservative*, September 16, 2022. As if social media wasn't already harmful

enough for your daughter._https://www.theameri-canconservative.com/pills-for-the-girls/

6. "Adolescents' recreational screen time doubled during pandemic, affecting mental health," University of California at San Francisco Department of Epidemiology and Biostatistics, November 21, 2021. The title says it all. https://epibiostat.ucsf.edu/news/adolescents%E2%80%99-recreational-screen-time-doubled-during-pandemic-affecting-mental-health

7. "Media Use Is Linked to Lower Psychological Well-Being: Evidence from Three Datasets." Another depressing National Library of Medicine Report. https://pubmed.ncbi.nlm.nih.gov/30859387/#:~:text=Heavy%20users%20(vs.,to%20report%20having%20attempted%20suicide

8. "An Overview of COPPA [The Children's Online Privacy Protection Act]" Electronic Protection Information Center (Epic.org). Epic.org is a superb on all children privacy matters. https://epic.org/issues/data-protection/childrens-privacy/

9. "How Technology Lowers Emotional Intelligence in Kids" by Sean Glover, July 14, 2017, *Psychology Today.* Glad the title is so subtle. https://www.psychologytoday.com/

us/blog/when-kids-call-the-shots/201707/
how-technology-lowers-emotional-intel-
ligence-in-kids#:~:text=Weakens%20
Self%2Dregulation,temper%20tantrums%20
and%20angry%20outbursts.

10. "How and When to Limit Kids' Tech Use," by
    Melanie Pinola, *The New York Times.* The title once
    again says it all. https://www.nytimes.com/guides/
    smarterliving/family-technology

11. "The Dark Psychology of Social Media: Why it
    feels like everything is going haywire," By Jonathan
    Haidt and Tobias Rose-Stockwell, December 2019,
    The Atlantic. More of Dr. Haidt's research brought
    to life. https://www.theatlantic.com/magazine/
    archive/2019/12/social-media-democracy/600763/

12. "Internet Addiction," Staff, *Psychology Today*,
    September 1, 2022. This is as plain as it gets on
    the danger of the glowing rectangle. Frightening.
    https://www.psychologytoday.com/us/basics/
    internet-addiction

13. "The top 10, 20, 30 Most Popular Apps for an-
    droid," Editors, ScreenTimeLabs.com, November
    2021. This article is good as is the website. From
    the founder: "Screen Time Labs, started, as you
    might guess, with screens and children. A dad
    (Steve) needed a way to reduce the time his three

kids used their new tablets that didn't involve him running a timer, nagging, or even worse, hiding their tablets." The site is packed with great advice like this piece: https://screentimelabs.com/blog/the-10-most-popular-apps-for-kids4.

14. "Top Apps Teens Are Using Right Now," Staff, besociallysmart.com. More information on the app world. https://besociallysmart.com/top-apps-teens/ https://www.waituntil8th.org/

15. https://www.waituntil8th.org - An entire site on cellphone nation. Here's the pitch: "Let kids be kids a little bit longer. This is for parents of young children, a wonderful website whose motto is: "We empower parents to say yes to waiting for the smartphone." The Wait Until 8th pledge empowers parents to rally together to delay giving children a smartphone until at least 8th grade. The FAQs and Blog are particularly useful sections.

Gamer Nation

This is a special section for those parents whose kids are literally and figuratively lost in the 10th Circle of video gaming – Fortnite, Call of Duty: Black Ops, Dead Rising, Assassin's Creed – you know, those wonderfully tame and moderate educational experiences. The following will be of help.

1. "10 Violent Video Games to Avoid," by Chad Sapieha and Jeana Lee Tahnk, *Parenting*. If this article doesn't make your blood run cold... https://www.parenting.com/activities/family-time/violent-video-games/

2. "Kids spending too much time gaming," By Dr. Ananya Mandal, *News on Medical And Life Sciences*, January 2020. The title says it all; tape this to your kid's hand-held console. https://www.news-medical.net/news/20200120/Kids-spending-too-much-time-gaming.aspx

3. "Resources to help you navigate the world of online video games, from setting parental controls to finding suitable games for your children," Staff, *Internetmatters.org*. A compendium of information on bad games and good parenting controls. https://www.internetmatters.org/resources/online-gaming-advice/online-gaming-resources/

An overall site for information on video gaming is the Digital Wellness Lab at Boston Children's Hospital - https://digitalwellnesslab.org/parents/video-games/

PRIVACY AND PREDATORS
Nellie Gut Check: The author begs, pleads and admonishes you to dig deep on these topics.

1. "18 Most Dangerous Social Media Apps" Editors, *Fenced.ai*, February 2022. Dangerous is a mild word… https://fenced.ai/ blogs/18-most-dangerous-social-media-apps/

2. "How do predators find children online?" Editors, The Beau Biden Foundation for the Protection of Children, June 2021. Good details on the defense against the pathologies of the pathological. https://www.beaubidenfoundation.org/ onlinepredatorsblog1/

3. "26 apps and websites favored by child predators - Are your kids using them?" Editors, Mosaic Technologies, May 12, 2022. This is a detailed look at where your kids shouldn't be.| https://experiencemosaic.com/the-top-apps-parents-should-know-their-kids-are-using/

4. "Websites and Apps to be Aware of: A Cheat Sheet For Parents," Editors, *Mental Health America*, February 2020 Again, direct and explanatory. https://www.mhanational.org/ websites-and-apps-be-aware-cheat-sheet-parents

5. "Secret Vault Apps That Hide Things on Your Kid's Phone," Editors, *NetNanny.com*, July 2020. Yes, it's come to this: The apps that hide apps. https://www. netnanny.com/blog/secret-vault-apps-that-hide-things-on-your-kid-e2-80-99s-phone/

6. "15 Best Apps To Hide Apps On Android & iOS 2020, techpout.com January 2020. This piece is for adults. And kids that are trying to hide something from adults. https://www.techpout.com/best-hide-apps-on-android-and-ios/

7. Online Safety, by Elana Pearl Ben-Joseph, MD, Nemours Health, August 2022. Good information all around. https://kidshealth.org/en/parents/net-safety.html

8. Internet safety: children 6-8 years, Editors, raisingChildren.net.au May 2021. Really good and extensive information on protecting kids from the Internet. https://raisingchildren.net.au/school-age/play-media-technology/online-safety/internet-safety-6-8-years

How Parents can control apps and the Internet

"The 10 Best Parental Control Apps and Services of 2022 / Apps and services for everything from limiting screen time to tracking locations," by Brad Stepheson, Lifewire.com August 2022. This is invaluable information, the go-to piece if you're interested in controlling your children's digital media usage. https://www.lifewire.com/best-parental-control-apps-4691864

And finally, a redundant list of the best Parental Phone and App Controls: Google Family Link, KidLogger, Qustodio, Bark, Nintendo Switch Parental Controls, Microsoft Family Safety, PlayStation Gamers: Family on PSN, Best Content Blocker Service: OpenDNS Family Shield.

FURTHER INFORMATION ON RESTORING CONFIDENCE AND WELL-BEING

OVERVIEW

This Appendix consolidates useful research and writings on the damaging effects of lockdowns with regards to the confidence and well-being of youth and was assembled to:

1. Provide you with background on the themes discussed in Chapter 3; and,

2. Offer you invaluable (yep, my word again) resources that will assist you in helping you ignite a confident, resilient child.

This first cite may surprise. For me, the most fearless commentator on building independence and character in youth is Lenore Skenazy. Yes, the woman noted in Chapter 3 as the tongue-in-cheek 'Worst Mom in America.'

Her site – www.LetGrow.org - is distinguished by the Skenazy mission:

"*When Adults Step Back, Kids Step Up.* At Let Grow, we believe today's kids are smarter and stronger than our culture gives them credit for. Treating them as physically and emotionally fragile is bad for their future — and ours."

Of note, her blog site is always updated and priceless: https://letgrow.org/library/

Here's the piece from *The New York Times* where she earned her distinction: "The Parenting Advice From 'America's Worst Mom,'" January 19, 2015. https://archive.nytimes.com/well.blogs.nytimes.com/2015/01/19/advice-from-americas-worst-mom/

Her book is a classic: *Free-Range Kids: How Parents and Teachers Can Let Go and Let Grow* (2021). "New York columnist-turned-movement leader Lenore Skenazy delivers a compelling and entertaining look at how we got so worried about everything our kids do, see, eat, read, wear, watch and lick -- and how to bid a whole lot of that anxiety goodbye. With real-world examples, advice, and a gimlet-eyed look at the way our culture forces fear down our throats, Skenazy describes how parents and educators can step back so kids step up. Positive change is faster, easier and a lot more fun than you'd believe. This is the book that has helped millions of American parents feel brave and optimistic again – and the same goes for their kids."

https://www.amazon.com/Free-Range-Kids-Parents-Teachers-Grow-dp-1119782147/dp/1119782147/ref=dp_ob_title_bk

---

Next up is Paul Tough, a contributing writer to the New York Times Magazine. Tough is the author, most recently, of The Inequality Machine: How College Divides Us and his three previous books include How Children Succeed: Grit, Curiosity, and the Hidden Power of Character, which was translated into 27 languages and spent more than a year on the New York Times hardcover and paperback best-seller lists. He is a speaker on topics including education, parenting,and student success.

I relied extensively relied upon Dr. Jean Twenge in Chapter 1 and her works in Appendix A. She belongs here as well. Her research on digital media, specifically social media, also contains wise words on GenZ and her notable definition of iGen, the cohort she has identified as growing up in a completely saturated digital world. On her website - www.JeanTwenge. com - is a particular useful section for parents: http://www. jeantwenge.com/faqs/

A fourth guru is Lauren Tamm who runs the site *The Military Wife and Mom*. (https://themilitarywifeandmom.com/). While the site content shades towards those families in the service, Tamm is solid when it comes to common sense commentary on kids and family life; she and her contributors offer a variety of perspectives from scientists, parents, coaches, and entrepreneurs. Her parenting page (https://themilitarywifeandmom.com/parenting-sub-homepage/) is an easy read. Better yet, it's from a Mom.

Last, another prominent figure in the world of parenting commentary is Josh Shipp, whose work can be found here: https://joshshipp.com/ Did I tell you he is a life force unto himself?!

"Statistically, Josh Shipp should be dead, in jail, or homeless. But his success as a preeminent author, speaker, and global youth empowerment expert is living proof of the power of one caring adult. A former at-risk foster kid turned youth advocate, Josh is renowned for the documentary TV series on A&E that followed his groundbreaking work with youth and families. Thanks to the support of teachers, counselors, and a wonderful set of foster parents, Josh went on to be listed on Inc. Magazine's 30 under 30 list and completed his postgraduate studies at Harvard."

He has written two national bestsellers to date, "<u>The Grown-Up's Guide to Teenage Humans</u>" — winner of the *Nautilus Gold Award for Parenting & Family* — and "<u>The Teen's Guide to World Domination</u>."

Useful articles on Reigniting Confidence and Mental Well-Being

Below is an array of various articles which I trust complement what you've read in Chapter 3.

1. "Laugh Out Loud: Use humor with your children and become a more playful parent," *Scholastic Parent*, August 2021. I am fully bought in on the value of humor in parenting; indeed, my previous (I won't inflict the tile upon you again) would give you the impression that parenting is a non-stop laugh fest. Humor grabs a kid's interest and it easily beats a tedious recitation of platitudes. https://www.scholastic.com/parents/family-life/social-emotional-learning/social-skills-for-kids/laugh-out-loud.html

2. "Encouraging Your Child's Sense of Humor," March of 2020, Staff of Children's Hospital of Minnesota. A quick read with a lasting message: "Laughing together is a way to connect, and a good sense of humor also can make kids smarter, healthier, and better able to cope with challenges." https://www.childrensmn.

org/educationmaterials/parents/article/10289/
encouraging-your-childs-sense-of-humor/

3. "12 Tips for Raising Confident Kids: How to build
    self-worth in children and help them feel they can
    handle what comes their way," Staff of The Child
    Mind Institute, April 2022. This is all soooo true:
    "Right from birth, kids learn new skills at a dizzy-
    ing rate. And along with those new abilities, they
    also acquire the confidence to use them. As chil-
    dren get older, that confidence can be as important
    as the skills themselves. It's by experiencing mas-
    tery and rebounding from failure that they develop
    healthy self-confidence."https://childmind.org/
    article/12-tips-raising-confident-kids/

4. "7 Parenting Tips on Building Self-Esteem and
    Self-Reliance in Young Children," Editorial Staff,
    Day2DayParenting.com, September 2021. This is a
    concise and thoughtful piece for parents whose kids
    need a shot of confidence. https://day2dayparenting.
    com/7-parenting-tips-on-building-self-esteem-and-
    self-reliance-in-young-children/

5. "Qualities of Good Parents for Tweens," by
    Rebecca Fraser-Thill, Verywellfamily.com, January
    18, 2022. Good suggestions on how to encour-
    age your kid, yes, in genuine, non-overboard
    fashion. https://www.verywellfamily.com/
    the-qualities-of-good-parents-3288421

6. "15 Tips to Build Self Esteem and Confidence in Teens" by Nicole Schwarz Biglifejournal.com, September 27, 2022 https://biglifejournal.com/blogs/blog/build-self-esteem-confidence-teens

7. "Boundaries, Routines and Early Bedtimes: 13 Habits That Raise Well-Adjusted Kids," by Lauren Tamm, TheMilitaryWifeAndMom.com, April 2022 https://themilitarywifeandmom.com/raise-well-adjusted-kid/

8. "Your Child's Self-Esteem," by D'Arcy Lyness, PhD, Nemours KidsHealth.com, November 2021 https://kidshealth.org/en/parents/self-esteem.html

9. "Family routines: how and why they work," Editors, RaisingChildren.net.au, June 2021. https://raisingchildren.net.au/grown-ups/family-life/routines-rituals-relationships/family-routines#:~:text=Routines%20help%20children%20feel%20safe,well%20planned%2C%20regular%20and%20predictable

10. "The Benefits of Chores," Editors, The Center for Parenting Education, August 2022. https://centerforparentingeducation.org/library-of-articles/responsibility-and-chores/part-i-benefits-of-chores/

11. "Why Children Need Chores / Doing household chores has many benefits—academically, emotionally

and even professionally," By Jennifer Wallace, *The Wall Street Journal*, March 13, 2015. https://www.wsj.com/articles/why-children-need-chores-1426262655

12. "Here's how to help your kids break out of their pandemic bubble and transition back to being with others" Editors, *The Conversation*, April 15, 2021 https://theconversation.com/heres-how-to-help-your-kids-break-out-of-their-pandemic-bubble-and-transition-back-to-being-with-others-157732

13. "Teaching Responsibility to Your Child," by Rebecca Fraser-Thill, verywellfamily.com, January 20, 2022. Good suggestions on how to your kid to step up when everyone else doesn't. https://www.verywellfamily.com/teaching-responsibility-to-your-child-3288496

14. "These Are the Best Self-help Books for Teenage Girls," by Ashley Ziegler, verywellfamily.com, April 19, 2022 https://www.verywellfamily.com/top-must-have-self-help-books-for-your-teenage-girl-2611380

15. "The 8 Best Inspirational Books for Teens of 2022" by Ashley Ziegler and Katrina Cossey, verywellfamily.com, April 11, 2022.https://www.verywellfamily.com/best-motivational-books-for-teens-4167093

16. "Dad Draws On Māori Roots To Raise 3 Resilient Sons. Step 1: Send Them On A Milk Run," By Michaeleen Doucleff, NPR, June 16, 2021. Yep, your not-so-humble author brings it in hot and fast (!). https://www.npr.org/sections/goatsandsoda/2021/06/19/1007836356/dad-draws-on-maori-roots-to-raise-3-resilient-sons-step-1-send-them-on-a-milk-ru

---

Last, two long-form, comprehensive articles that explore further the devastating effect of lockdowns on the mental well-being of youth.

"Worldwide increases in adolescent loneliness" December 2021, National Library of Medicine. Drs. Twenge and Haidt are among the coauthors of this broad study. https://pubmed.ncbi.nlm.nih.gov/34294429/

"The lost boys of Covid: School closures have set off a devastating domino effect" August 24, 2022, *Spectator World*, by Bethany Mandel. A long, thoughtful piece on what else? The impact of school closures. https://spectatorworld.com/topic/the-lost-boys-of-covid-school-closures/

TEACHING GRATITUDE

Below are some tips for teaching Gratitude from First Things First.

Nellie Check: I'm one of the most unsentimental men you'll ever meet and I think the below are priceless.

1. Teach them to say thank you to the people who do things for them. That can be their server at a restaurant, a brother or sister who helps them pick up toys, or a friend who gives them a birthday gift.

2. Tell your kids why you are grateful for them. Be specific in letting your children know they are special and loved. For example: 'I appreciate the way you help your brother tie his shoes.'

3. Talk about the things you are grateful for. This can be done in many ways, from a blessing before dinner to keeping a family gratitude journal.

4. Support a charitable event or organization. Whether you are donating clothes or toys, participating in a food drive, or baking cookies for a new neighbor, talk to children about what those actions mean to those who receive the kindness.

5. Be consistent. Like all skills, gratitude is not learned in one lesson.

Your child's first five years are a great opportunity to help them develop the skills they need to be successful later in life. Research shows that thankful people are usually more optimistic. They're also less depressed and stressed. So, when we teach our children to appreciate what they have, and what others do for them, we are helping them become happier, healthier adults. https://www.firstthingsfirst.org/first-things/teaching-young-kids-about-gratitude/

University of North Carolina at Chapel Hill / The Raising Grateful Children program.

"We developed this program to provide parents and caretakers with skills to foster gratitude in their children, particulary pre-teens and teens. We know there are many ways to foster gratitude in children and that these skills may not be the best fit for everyone. We hope that you accept them in the spirit in which they are offered – as another tool for your growing parent toolbox. Thanks for your interest in our program and in joining us for this adventure in parenting."

https://hussong.web.unc.edu/gratitude-conversations-program/

VARIOUS ARTICLES ON THE EFFECTS OF PANDEMIC LOCKDOWN

1. "CDC study: Abuse, violence, other events linked to poor mental health in teens during COVID pandemic," by Adrianna Rodriguez, *USAToday*, October 14, 2022. That's right: A CDC study examining the devastating effects of CDC mandates. https://www.usatoday.com/story/news/health/2022/10/13/cdc-teens-report-poor-mental-health-during-covid/10475159002/

2. The full CDC Report is here: https://www.cdc.gov/mmwr/volumes/71/wr/mm7141a2.htm?s_cid=mm7141a2_w

3. "Loneliness and mental health in children and adolescents with pre-existing mental health problems: A rapid systematic review," by Emily Hards, Maria Elizabeth Loades, Nina Higson-Sweeney, and Roz Shafran, National Library of Medicine, June 6, 2022 https://pubmed.ncbi.nlm.nih.gov/34529837/#:~:text=Conclusions%3A%20Loneliness%20is%20associated%20with,this%20relationship%20may%20be%20bidirectional.

4. "Rapid Systematic Review: The Impact of Social Isolation and Loneliness on the Mental Health of Children and Adolescents in the Context of COVID-19" by Maria Elizabeth Loades, Eleanor

Chatburn, Nina Higson-Sweeney, Shirley Reynolds, and Roz Shafran, National Library of Medicine, November 20, 2020. https://www.ncbi.nlm.nih. gov/pmc/articles/PMC7267797/

5. "Pediatricians, Child and Adolescent Psychiatrists and Children's Hospitals Declare National Emergency in Children's Mental Health," Press Release, October 19, 2021, American Academy of Pediatrics (AAP), the American Academy of Child and Adolescent Psychiatry (AACAP) and the Children's Hospital Association (CHA). https://www.aacap.org/aacap/ zLatest_News/Pediatricians_CAPs_Childrens_ Hospitals_Declare_National_Emergency_ Childrens_Mental_Health.aspx

6. "Children's mental health issues have increased, insurance claims suggest," By Chia-Yi Hou, *The Hill*, September 12, 2022. https://thehill. com/changing-america/well-being/mental- health/3634774-childrens-mental-health-issues-have- increased-insurance-claims-suggest/

7. "COVID-19 has made children more worried, scared, and lonely," by Connor Ibettson, January 21, 2020, YouGov UK poll. https://yougov.co.uk/ topics/health/articles-reports/2021/01/12/covid- 19-has-made-children-more-worried-scared-and

8. "It's a crisis: More children suffering mental health issues, challenges of the pandemic," by Joan Murray, *CBS News*, Aug. 1, 2022. https://www.cbsnews.com/miami/news/crisis-more-children-suffering-mental-health-issues-challenges-pandemic/

9. "The Case Against Masks for Children: It's abusive to force kids who struggle with them to sacrifice for the sake of unvaccinated adults," by Marty Makary and H. Cody Meissner, Aug. 8, 2021, *The Wall Street Journal*. https://www.wsj.com/articles/masks-children-parenting-schools-mandates-covid-19-coronavirus-pandemic-biden-administration-cdc-11628432716

10. "'A cry for help': CDC warns of a steep decline in teen mental health / More than 4 in 10 told the health agency they felt 'persistently sad or hopeless'", by Moriah Balingit, *The Washington Post*, March 13, 2022 https://www.washingtonpost.com/education/2022/03/31/student-mental-health-decline-cdc/

11. "Randi Weingarten Flunks the Pandemic / National test results reveal the damage from school closures,' Editorial Board, *The Wall Street Journal*, September 1, 2022. https://www.wsj.com/articles/randi-weingarten-flunks-the-pandemic-naep-test-scores-decline-schools-covid-american-federation-of-teachers-11662069418 ;

12. "Kids Are Far, Far Behind in School / Educators need a plan ambitious enough to remedy enormous learning losses," By Thomas Kane, Director of the Center for Education Policy Research at Harvard University, *The Atlantic,* May 22, 2022. https://www.theatlantic.com/ideas/archive/2022/05/schools-learning-loss-remote-covid-education/629938/

Websites worth a look:

https://girlsthriving.com/ - "Raising Confident, Capable and Connected Girls. The resources on this website will help you nurture the social and emotional well-being of your daughter."

https://www.rachelsimmons.com/about/ - "My programs help girls and women amplify their voices, communicate with confidence, and build their resilience." Ms. Simmons is the co-founder of the national nonprofit Girls Leadership. She is the author *The Curse of the Good Girl: Raising Girls with Courage and Confidence,* and *Enough As She Is.*

https://www.parents.com/ - "At Parents, our mission is simple—to provide you with trustworthy advice and a supportive community as you raise the next generation of confident and compassionate kids. Parenthood is rewarding, but we all know it's not always easy—and it definitely comes with a lot of questions. Since 1926, Parents has been committed to supporting caregivers through every step of the parenting journey—from those big life decisions to the memory-making moments."

https://yourteenmag.com/ - "Parenting can get lonely when kids get older and the playgroups fade away. The glossy magazines usually focus on young kids, and we may find ourselves looking for new sources of answers to our parenting questions and concerns." Plus, more than ever, we want to feel like we're not alone. Friends Stephanie Silverman and Susan Borison saw that, like themselves, other parents of teenagers were hungry for expert advice and nonjudgmental support. In 2007, we founded Your Teen Media to meet this need."

Finally, to aggregate, below are two links to suggested parenting websites:

"Top parenting resources from psychologists / These scientifically supported sites, programs and books are among psychology's best for helping parents raise their kids" by Amy Novetney, American Psychological Association, August 2018

https://www.apa.org/monitor/2018/04/parenting-resources

"9 Popular Parenting Websites for Successfully Raising Teenagers ? Every parent wants to overcome minor problems and strengthen their relationship with their kids. If you want to handle difficult situations and topics, these websites are great starting points" by Sandy Writtenhouse, MakeUseOf.com, August 2017

https://www.makeuseof.com/tag/popular-parenting-websites-teenagers/

BOOKS

Noted above are a range of books to which I would add these three below...

Make Your Bed: Little Things That Can Change Your Life...And Maybe the World by Admiral William H. McRaven.

"Should be read by every leader in America... it's a book to inspire your children and grandchildren to become everything that they can. It is a book to discuss with your executive leadership team as a spur to meeting shared goals. Most of all, it is a book that will leave you with tears in your eyes." *The Wall Street Journal*, Sept. 2019

https://www.amazon.com/Make-Your-Bed-Little-Things/dp/1455570249

When Kids Call the Shots: How to Seize Control from Your Darling Bully--and Enjoy Parenting Again by Sean Glover. Glover's book was named Best New Nonfiction from Publishers Weekly and was included on *The New York Times* recommended reading list for parents.

https://www.amazon.com/When-Kids-Call-Shots-Control/dp/0814436005

Rich Dad Poor Dad: What the Rich Teach Their Kids About Money That the Poor and Middle Class Do Not! by Robert T. Kiyosaki

https://www.amazon.com/gp/product/1612680194/ref=as_li_tl?ie=UTF8&camp=1789&creative=9325&creativeASIN=1612680194&linkCode=as2&tag=projectboldli-20&linkId=8816826bc83c9992eefe90763ed1784e

ADDITIONAL MATERIAL ON PHYSICAL HEALTH

OVERVIEW

This Appendix consolidates useful research and writings on child nutrition and physical activity and was assembled to:

1. Provide you with additional information on the themes discussed in Chapter 4; and,

2. Offer you invaluable (yep, my word yet again) resources that will assist you will developing a healthy and physically active child.

GETTING YOUR KID IN SHAPE

1. "10 tips to get kids to exercise / By encouraging your children to exercise every day, you can help them

maintain a healthy weight and help prevent diseases like cancer later in life," MD Anderson Health Center, August 2014. Useful and timeless advice on how to get your kid moving again. https://www. mdanderson.org/publications/focused-on-health/ tips-to-get-kids-to-exercise.h17-1589046.html

2. The amazing Michele Obama and her "Let's Move! campaign - "America's move to raise a healthier generation of kids." The information here is priceless, timeless, and ideal for parents. https://letsmove. obamawhitehouse.archives.gov/

3. BONUS! As part of the Let's Move campaign, Michele Obama and Ellen DeGeneres dancing on *The Ellen Show.* Use your google machine to find this link: https://www.youtube.com/ watch?v=UZO5q0B5wfw

4. "Kids Exercise List for the Classroom or Home," YourTherapySource.com, August 2022. This is a *superb* breakdown of all the exercise your kid – and YOU – can do at home with little space and no equipment needed. https://www.yourtherapysource. com/blog1/2022/05/26/kids-exercise-list/

5. Fun Workouts For Kids And Adults," Staff, Rebounderz.com, April 2017. More great tips on *getting the whole family involved.* https://www.rebounderz.com/fun-workouts-kids-adults/

6. "Physical Activity Guidelines for School-Aged Children and Adolescents," CDC, July 2022. This gives an overview of the kind and types of exercise your kids should be getting. https://www.cdc.gov/healthyschools/physicalactivity/guidelines.htm#:~:text=The%20Physical%20Activity%20Guidelines%20for,to%2Dvigorous%20physical%20activity%20daily.

7. "The Pandemic Within the Pandemic: Childhood Obesity," Dr. Julie Snethen, Director of the PhD program at the UWM College of Nursing, and Cindy Greenberg, Dean of the College of Health and Human Development at California State University, Fullerton. Good facts and good advice on how restore your kid's physical health. https://www.wisconsin.edu/all-in-wisconsin/story/pandemic-within-a-pandemic-childhood-obesity-rises-during-covid-shutdown/

What they should eat

1. "Dietary Guidelines for Americans," U.S. Department of Agriculture, August 2022. Here it is, folks. Following these suggestions is simple. https://www.nal.usda.gov/legacy/fnic/dietary-guidelines

2. "The 19 Best Vegetables for Kids," Else Nutrition, July 2021. This gives detailed information on the list

found in Chapter 5. https://elsenutrition.com/blogs/news/19-best-vegetables-for-kids

3. "Top 10 fruits good for kids" HealthBeginsWithMom.com, July 2021. Simple advice from a Mom – does it get more credible than that?! https://www.healthbeginswithmom.com/top-10-fruits-good-kids/

4. "The 10 Best Foods for Kids" by Vincent Iannelli, MD, VeryWellFamily.com June 2020. Not everything is fruit and vegetables. This is a straightforward guide to basic, healthy food for your child. https://www.verywellfamily.com/best-foods-for-kids-2633967

VARIOUS ARTICLES ON LOCKDOWNS AND HEALTH

1. "Children, Obesity, and COVID-19," Centers for Disease Control and Prevention (CDC), June 2022. At this link is a sobering overview of overweight and obese children. It's an active page with useful and quite detailed suggestions for parents on diet and exercise. https://www.cdc.gov/obesity/data/childhood.html

2. "Rates of New Diagnosed Cases of Type 1 and Type 2 Diabetes Continue to Rise Among Children, Teens." CDC, Updated February 2022. This is also a useful link, offering detailed advice on diabetes prevention

and control. https://www.cdc.gov/diabetes/research/reports/children-diabetes-rates-rise.html

3. "Changes in Body Mass Index Among Children and Adolescents During the COVID-19 Pandemic," Research Letter, August 2021. This is a scholarly paper evaluating pandemic-related (read: pandemic lockdowns) changes in weight in school-aged youths; good and detailed background. https://jamanetwork.com/journals/jama/fullarticle/2783690

4. "Screen Time Increases Teenagers' Incidence of Overweight and Obesity," Editors, *Physician's Weekly*, May 2022. https://www.physiciansweekly.com/screen-time-increases-teenagers-incidence-of-overweight-and-obesity/

NELLIE'S NOTES ON EDUCATION

OVERVIEW

This Appendix is a consolidation of the most timely and incisive writings on the educational losses suffered by kids as result of lockdowns that forced school closures.

I have a singular view on education and if you'd like to hear it please email me at Jeff@ResilientSons.com

---

Below is a collection of articles serving as background for this book.

1. "Online School Put U.S. Kids Behind. Some Adults Have Regrets," by Bianca Toness & Jocelyn Gecke, RealClearPolitics.com, October 24, 2022. https://www.realclearpolitics.com/articles/2022/10/24/

online_school_put_us_kids_behind_some_adults_
have_regrets_148365.html

2. "Private Schooling after a Year of COVID-19," by Neal McCluskey, Cato Institute, April 21, 2021. Provides a good overall view of the pros and cons of secondary school education dealing with lockdowns. https://www.cato.org/policy-analysis/private-schooling-after-year-covid-19-how-private-sector-has-fared-how-keep-it#introduction1.

3. "A cry for help': CDC warns of a steep decline in teen mental health: More than 4 in 10 told the health agency they felt 'persistently sad or hopeless,'" by Moriah Balingit, *The Washington Post*, March 31, 2022 – a tough look at how kids suffer when society in most of its forms is arbitrarily shut down. https://www.washingtonpost.com/education/2022/03/31/student-mental-health-decline-cdc/

4. "Fauci Claims He Had 'Nothing to Do' With School Closures. His Own Statements Suggest Otherwise." by John Miltimore, FEE, October 23, 2022 https://fee.org/articles/fauci-claims-he-had-nothing-to-do-with-school-closures-his-own-statements-suggest-otherwise/

5. "Sorry Seems to Be the Hardest Word," by Jeffery Tucker, Brownstone Institute, October

22, 2022. https://brownstone.org/articles/
sorry-seems-to-be-the-hardest-word/

6. "ACT Test Scores Drop to Lowest in 30 Years
   Following School Closures," by Cheyanne
   Mumphrey, Associated Press, October 13,
   2022. https://www.realclearpolitics.com/arti-
   cles/2022/10/13/act_test_scores_drop_to_lowest_
   in_30_years_following_school_closures_148318.
   html

7. "Randi Weingarten Flunks the Pandemic / National
   test results reveal the damage from school closures," by the Editorial Board, *The Wall Street Journal*,
   September 1, 2022. A revealing and tragic look at
   two decades of progress reversed. https://www.wsj.
   com/articles/randi-weingarten-flunks-the-pandem-
   ic-naep-test-scores-decline-schools-covid-american-
   federation-of-teachers-11662069418

8. "Kids Are Far, Far Behind in School" by Thomas
   Kane, Director of the Center for Education Policy
   Research at Harvard University, *The Atlantic*, May
   22, 2022. A statistical dive into how school closures
   and remote education didn't work. https://www.
   theatlantic.com/ideas/archive/2022/05/schools-
   learning-loss-remote-covid-education/629938/

9. "Seismic Learning Loss Is a National Crisis. But does
   the US have the political will to fix it?" by Michael

R. Bloomberg, *The Washington Post*, September 14, 2022. Whatever you think of Mike Bloomberg, he's right on in this piece. https://www.washingtonpost.com/business/pandemic-learning-loss-is-a-national-crisis/2022/09/14/6d2a9706-340c-11ed-a0d6-415299bfebd5_story.html

10. "Parents were demonized for demanding schools reopen sooner. Now, we know they were right, by Mary Vought, *USA Today*, October 1, 2022. "With the learning losses they have suffered, students could pay the price for school boards' wrong-headed decisions for years, if not decades, to come." Whoa. https://www.iwf.org/2022/10/01/parents-were-demonized-for-demanding-schools-reopen-sooner-now-we-know-they-were-right/

11. "America has a problem. We, my fellow progressives, must admit it," by Jill Filipovic, *CNN Online*, September 6, 2022. https://www.cnn.com/2022/09/06/opinions/covid-school-closures-problem-filipovic/index.html

12. "It's back-to-school time, and the culture chasm is wider than ever," by Larry Sand, *American Greatness*, September 16, 2022. General observations about schools and culture post-lockdowns. https://amgreatness.com/2022/09/16/the-education-revolution-rages-on/

13. "School Choice Rising: Parental discontent with public education has sparked new momentum for alternatives" by Steve Malanga, City Journal, Summer 2022. A dispassionate look at school choice and private institutions in the wake of school closures. https://www.city-journal.org/school-choice-rising

Author Bio

Jeff Nelligan is the father of three boys and a well-known commentator in the world of American parenting. *Rebound* is a sequel to his prior book, *Four Lessons From My Three Sons: How You Can Raise A Resilient Kid*, which details how he helped guide his sons through childhood to the U.S. Naval Academy, Williams College, and West Point. *Four Lessons* spent four months on the top-20 Amazon's Parenting Best Sellers list and was the subject of feature stories on National Public Radio and in dozens of parenting publications, including: *Parents Magazine, Fatherly, Young Teen Magazine, The Good Men Project, Fatherhood* and *LetGrow*.

Currently a public affairs executive in Washington, D.C., Nelligan formerly worked for three Members of the U.S. Congress and served twice as a Presidential appointee. An Army veteran, he is a of Polynesian ancestry (Māori Indian, New Zealand) and a graduate of Williams College and Georgetown University Law School. His website is www.NelliganBooks. com and he can be reached at Jeff@ResilientSons.com.

FOUR LESSONS FROM MY THREE SONS

HOW YOU CAN RAISE RESILIENT KIDS

JEFF NELLIGAN

Made in USA - Kendallville, IN
83484_9798360844747
12.13.2022 1424